# THE
## 12-VOLT
## BIBLE

# THE 12-VOLT BIBLE

## by Miner K. Brotherton

*Drawings by Michael Blaser*

**Seven Seas Press, Inc.**
*Newport, Rhode Island*

Published by Seven Seas Press, Inc., Newport, R.I. 02840

**Library of Congress Cataloging in Publication Data**
Brotherton, Miner K., 1929–
    The 12-volt Bible.
    1. Boats and boating—Electric equipment.    I. Title.
II.  Title: The twelve-volt Bible.
VM325.B76    1985        623.8′503          84-13934
ISBN 0-915160-81-1


1   3   5   7   9    0   8   6   4   2


Designed by Irving Perkins Associates
Printed in the United States of America
Edited by James R. Gilbert

*I dedicate this book to my first mate
of many years, Shirley,
a loving wife, a caring mother, an
ideal cruising companion,
and a willing participant in all my life's
activities. But best of all, she puts
up with me.*

# Acknowledgments

Few people can accomplish much entirely on their own. Most of us are dependent on many others. I take this opportunity to thank all those who over the years have tried to teach me about electricity. In particular I thank Dr. R. Marshall Helms, retired Professor of Physics at East Carolina University, who taught the practical aspects of electricity as well as the theoretical in his classes, and showed me how to do so many things when I worked in his shop.

I thank the Battery Council International for providing me with much useful information about the construction, operation, servicing, and maintenance of storage batteries, and for allowing me to reproduce their illustrations. I thank the various manufacturers of marine electrical products and devices who have generously supplied me with information and illustrations. Without their help, this project would have been much more difficult.

I thank my friends who have in recent years encouraged me to write about marine topics, especially Allan Vaitses and Tom Colvin, and Herb Gliick who gave me the opportunity to do it regularly in *OFFSHORE: NEW ENGLAND'S BOATING MAGAZINE*, and paid me, too. I thank the editors of *CRUISING WORLD* for their encouragement in selecting and publishing some of my articles, and I thank Jim Gilbert of SEVEN SEAS PRESS for asking me to do this book.

Miner K. Brotherton

# CONTENTS

## CHAPTER 4
# THE WIRING   Electrical Veins And Arteries                51

## CHAPTER 5
# THE CONTROLS   Brains Of The System                67

# Introduction

Welcome aboard the *12-Volt Bible*. Basically, this is a nuts and bolts primer, an elementary textbook for boat owners who are not skilled electricians.

By profession, I am a teacher of physical science. By choice I am a boat owner, marine writer, scientist, boatbuilder, environmentalist, confirmed cruiser, licensed vessel operator, one-time boat salesman, and former airplane and helicopter mechanic and flight crew member. But most of all, I like to just plain mess around with boats. That includes doing all my own work on board our Colvin-designed gaff schooner which my wife and I completed from a custom fiberglass hull and deck by Al Vaitses; so I have had to teach myself lots of different skills, including boat electricity.

In doing this I have relied on the printed work of many others. No one is born with electrical knowledge; you have to learn it someplace. However, I have found that some books like this are written by engineers who seem to forget that most of us are lawyers, accountants, English teachers, psychologists, and musicians. What do we know about power factors, zener diodes, and squirrel cage rotors? Some others start out very basic, but soon become super-sophisticated in subject matter. Without my background in physics and physical science, I'm sure I would not have been able to follow all their explanations.

Of course, there is no guarantee you will be able to follow all of mine, but at least I will remember who most of your are, to make this a book you will want to carry on-board with you.

I won't show you how to repair your Loran or install a radar; but I will tell you how your 12-volt DC electrical system works, what you should do to maintain it in good operating condition, how to recognize when you have an electrical problem, how to troubleshoot to locate the problem, what simple tools and techniques you'll need to fix common electrical system problems.

Some complex problems are just better left to professionals. But when your running lights quit while you're crossing a shipping lane 50 miles from the nearest marina, it is essential to know where to look to try to get them working again. If this little book helps to accomplish that, then the effort put into it will have been worthwhile, and you will have invested your money wisely.

# Preface
## A FEW WORDS OF CAUTION

Right up front here, I should say a few words about precautions and hazards. I know the title indicates our coverage will be limited to 12 volts DC, but that does not mean that we can treat the system with a cavalier attitude. Even though we can get 12 volts from a handful of AA flashlight cells (eight, to be exact), this does not imply in any way that we can ignore basic safety standards and practices, which are prescribed by such organizations as the American Boat and Yacht Council, Inc. and the National Fire Protection Association. There is good reason for these high standards—survival—your survival and the survival of your boating companions. Safety and survival are the names of the game.

An overloaded, unprotected circuit can generate tremendous heat, which may melt the wire's insulation or even start a fire. An arcing switch, relay, or motor can ignite explosive vapors that may have collected in the bilge or any closed compartment, with disastrous results. Electrical leaks and stray electric currents can destroy a boat or its equipment by electrolysis. It is true that you are much less likely to be shocked by your boat's electrical system than you are by your house wiring or by the marina shore power box on your slip, but there is a lot more to safety than avoiding shocks.

Most of the hazards associated with our system can be found in the battery compartment. If you have ever accidentally dropped a screwdriver or long wrench on a storage battery so that it hit both posts or terminals you know what I mean— sparks fly and the tool has a permanent gouge or two at the points of contact where the metal melted away. Or maybe you saw the sparks fly while you were hooking up a pair of jumper cables to start your car when its battery was down. Even though

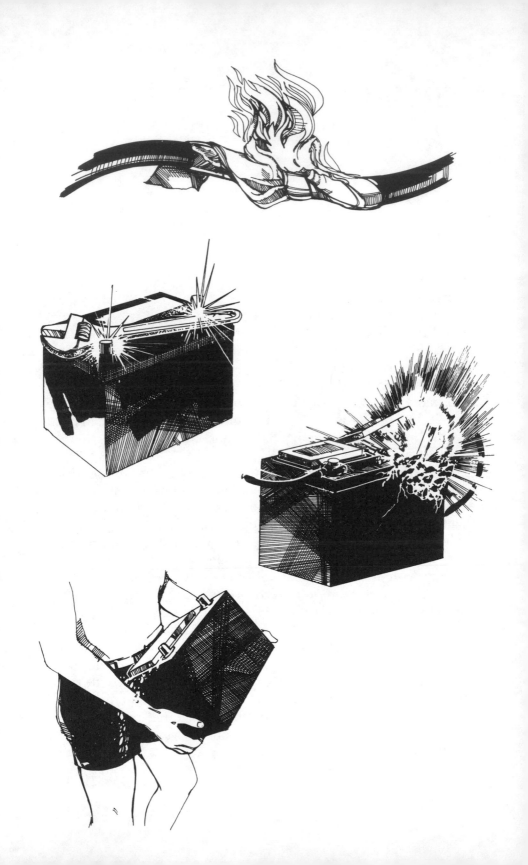

there is only 12 volts, very large currents and significant energy is involved.

While your batteries are being charged, especially near the end of the charging cycle, oxygen and hydrogen gases are produced from the electrical dissociation of water. They form a particularly hazardous explosive mixture if allowed to accumulate in a confined space aboard. A single spark under the right conditions could trigger a boat-and-flesh-damaging explosion.

Finally, there is the hazard of the battery electrolyte, a sulfuric acid solution. Spill it on your clothes and it will eat holes in them. Spill it on your skin and you'll get severe burns unless it's washed off immediately and neutralized with an alkaline solution such as baking soda (sodium bicarbonate). Spilling the acid in your eyes can lead to blindness or severely impaired vision. Be especially careful with your eyes. Don't look closely into the filler holes to check for liquid level while the battery is charging; a rising bubble can easily pop and splash acid into your eyeball. Use a flashlight and look from a distance. Use eye protection goggles or glasses whenever possible. These are grim scenarios, I know. I am trying to frighten you a little bit, but only to make you aware of the potential hazards. A 12-volt DC system is NOT inherently safe. It is RELATIVELY safe, but it does demand your attention and your respect.

# THE
# 12-VOLT
# BIBLE

## CHAPTER 1

# BASIC THEORY OF ELECTRICITY

## THE ATOM AND ITS ELECTRONS

It should stand to reason that if ever we hope to comprehend how our boat's electrical system works, we must have some knowledge of the basic theory behind it. Unfortunately, electricity almost defies description. It is fairly easy to say how it behaves, what it does and does not do, and how we use it; but because we cannot see, touch, taste, smell, or hear electricity, it appears all the more mysterious to us.

### THE ATOM

In order to trace this elusive stuff, we have to start with the atom—the basic building block of every element—because that's where electricity begins. As strange as it may sound at first, an atom consists mostly of empty space—even the heaviest and the hardest of atoms. This space is very sparsely occupied by electrons, protons and neutrons. In simplest terms, electrons are the smallest quantities of electricity, and for purposes of this book are regarded as *particles*. The central core of the atom consists of protons and neutrons, which provide most of the mass of the atom. Each neutron (uncharged) and each

3

proton (one positive charge per proton) weighs about 1,800 times as much as an electron, which carries a charge equal and opposite to that of the proton; i.e., it is negatively charged. Again without getting too fancy about it, let's just say that the electron is in an orbit of rather large radius. The atoms of the various elements, such as hydrogen, oxygen, lead, iron and so on, contain characteristic numbers of these particles; that's what distinguishes one from another. Hydrogen is the simplest; it owns just one proton and one electron orbiting around it. Moreover, this electron can be pulled away under the right conditions, leaving a bare proton with its positive charge. This is now called a positive "ion," while the flight of the electron up, up, and away constitutes an electric current.

HYDROGEN          LITHIUM          NITROGEN

Figure 1–1

These sketches cannot do justice to scale. Imagine a domed football stadium with a ball bearing sitting on the 50-yard line and some mosquitoes flying around the rafters. The ball bearing is the nucleus and the mosquitoes are the electrons—almost to proper scale!

## ELECTRONS

It's those little, nearly massless, negative charges that whirl about the nucleus at extremely high speeds—in certain orbits or "energy levels"—those mosquitoes in the rafters, that we are interested in. The electron is the basic "grain" or unit of electricity, and all electrons belong to atoms. All electrons are identical, no matter which kind of atom they come from. Each has the same amount of negative electrical charge and the same little bit of mass. Atoms themselves are always electrically neutral; that is, they have just as many positive charges in the nucleus as they do negative electrons whirling about them. If an atom, or group of atoms, loses or gains one or more electrons, it becomes charged, either positively or negatively, and is then called an "ion."

## MOLECULES AND BONDING

Atoms join themselves together to form larger structures called "molecules"; these may involve the same or different kinds of atoms. Molecules are held together by the electrons rather than by the nuclei, and the name given to the holding mechanism is "bonding." Electrons are arranged in several different configurations in order to accomplish the bonding function.

If an electron is actually transferred from one atom to another, the bond is called *ionic*. Of course this means that both atoms become ions as soon as the transfer occurs. One gains an electron to become a negative ion, and the other loses an electron to become a positive ion; the resulting attractive force between them makes this an extremely strong bond. Should this molecule ever separate, the ions are already there. Most salts, including common table salt, the major dissolved constituent of sea water, are held together with ionic bonds.

Sometimes two or more atoms are held together by a sharing of one or more of the outermost electrons. Now these electrons will orbit about the whole group, rather than their own home base-atom, and thus "glue" it all together. Such bonding is called *covalent*. When either covalent or ionic molecules dissociate, or come apart, in a solution, they separate into two subgroups, each having the opposite charge. Thus $H_2SO_4$, sulfuric acid, in our battery becomes 2 H($+$) and $SO_4$ (2$-$). Later we'll see why that is important. When ions move, they carry their respective charges with them. This is what constitutes the electric current inside a storage battery.

Atoms that make up our copper wires also share electrons, but in a different way. When a metal solidifies from a molten state, the atoms are locked together in what is called a crystalline structure. They are jam-packed so closely together that their electron orbits overlap, forming what is sometimes called an "electron cloud." Individual electrons no longer belong to specific atoms or groups of atoms; they belong to the whole crystal in the *metallic bond*. The crystal remains electrically neutral, having just as many plus charges as minus ones, but now this cloud of electrons is free to migrate throughout the length of the wire, hooking up with whichever atoms it happens to be near. These are the "free electrons" that make some materials such as copper and silver very good conductors of electric current. Other substances, lacking them, are poor conductors often called "insulators."

### IONS AND ELECTRONS

In our boat's electrical system we usually find the ions in the battery and electrons in the wires. Chemical reactions take place in the battery that involve the movement of the ions through the liquid electrolyte. As a result of these reactions, electrons enter and leave the ends of the wires and move very quickly around the circuit inside the wires. With a stopwatch, you cannot measure the time between flipping a switch and seeing a bulb light up; it would be only one-hundred-millionth of a second for a 10-foot piece of wire. The electrons don't travel that fast, but the electrical event does. That's because the wire already has lots of those "free electrons" in it. You might liken it to a soda straw completely full of small BB's. Now if you shove one more BB into one end, another will immediately jump out the far end, but it's not the same BB that traveled all the way through the straw. In our boat's electric circuits the electron cloud is set into motion when a voltage is applied to the ends of the conductor. That creates a current. Now we'll have to see what those terms mean.

## TERMS DEFINED

### COULOMB'S LAW

A basic rule of electricity says that unlike charges (+ and −) attract each other, and like charges, either (+ and +, or − and −) repel each other.

*The force of attraction or repulsion between charged bodies is directly proportional to the product of the charges on the bodies and inversely proportional to the square of the distance between them.*

This law dates back to 1789 when the French scientist Charles Coulomb did the original research in the field of static electricity—charges at rest. We're interested in moving charges —current electricity, but Coulomb's Law still applies, even though we won't have to use it for any calculations. That's really about all the theory we need to know in order to begin.

## CHARGE

Let's begin with *charge.* The ultimate piece of electricity is the electron, and charge measures how many electrons we're talking about. It is a quantity measure, like a ream of paper, so that's why it is always abbreviated "Q." *Coulomb* is the charge unit, equal to six and a quarter billion—billion electrons. Fortunately, no one ever has to count them. Besides, we never need to use this unit by itself in boat electricity. It is only when charges start moving that we begin to take notice.

## CURRENT

The rate at which charge moves is called *current.* Now that *is* important to boat electricity. We measure electric current in *amperes,* but everyone says amps. By definition, a current of 1 ampere exists in a circuit when 1 coulomb of charge is passing a point every second. Current is the flow rate, just as in a river. Current is always abbreviated "I." So we could say in mathematical shorthand, $I = Q/T$, which means:

*Current is equal to the amount of charge that moves past a point in a given time interval.*

In some cases the time is more important than the amount of charge. In a lightning discharge, for instance, tremendous currents may be involved, even though the total amount of charge transferred might not be so large at all. The lightning event is over in a few thousandths of a second (milliseconds), so when we divide the charge by a very small time interval, we get an enormous result for the lightning current—values of 60,000 to 100,000 amperes are not uncommon. On your boat, most circuits will have considerably less than 20 amps in them; but not all. Your engine starter circuit can give you a real surprise. Starting currents can be as high as 800 amps for cranking a cold diesel in winter! A warm summer gas engine will draw 150 to 250 amps while starting.

### VOLTAGE, POTENTIAL DIFFERENCE, AND EMF

*Voltage,* or *potential,* is what pushes the electrons through the wires around the circuit. It may be thought of as acting similarly to pressure in a water system—the higher the pressure, the more gallons of water will flow from the hose per minute. The higher the voltage, the greater the current in the wires. Potential is also related to energy in a circuit in this way: Potential = energy/charge, where the energy is measured in *joules.* This is of more interest to theoreticians than to boat owners, but it will help us define some other terms. Potential is measured in *volts,* hence its more common name of voltage, and it is usually abbreviated "V." In our 12-volt system, each coulomb of charge in the current carries 12 joules of energy around the circuit and expends them in doing work. That's because of the way we define the volt:

---

*One volt of potential is equal to one joule of energy per coulomb of charge.*

---

Acutally it is the *potential difference* between any two points in the circuit that pushes the charges along; and if there is no difference in potential between two points, there won't be any current. Now we know how a bird can sit on a high voltage power line without being electrocuted—both feet are at the same potential, side by side, the difference is zero and so is the current. But if the bird stretches its wings far enough to touch another wire at a diffferent potential—ZAP! Just like the back-yard bug killers.

*EMF* stands for *electro-motive-force,* also measured in volts. EMF differs from voltage in that EMF always applies to a source of energy, called a *seat.* On our boat we have two seats of EMF—the battery and the alternator. In any circuit, the seat's function is to maintain a potential difference between the ends of the circuit to cause the current to flow. The seat sup-plies energy to the charges as they leave it, and the charges dissipate the energy as they travel around the circuit. Another rule of electricity says that the EMF supplied by the seat must be exactly used up as voltage drops around the circuit. Some-times EMF is abbreviated "E" to keep it separated from volt-age "V," even though both are measured in volts. In our water analogy, a seat of EMF would be like a pump, constantly lifting the water at one end to maintain pressure to cause the water to flow through the pipes.

## ENERGY

We have already mentioned electric energy in defining the volt. Let's look at it a little more closely, and see if we can't find some other more common units for it than joules, which is not a frequently-used term. The joule is not a huge energy unit. It is nearly the same as the work you would do in lifting a pound weight nine inches; so a joule is about ¾ of a foot-pound. En-ergy and work are interchangeable. Energy makes it possible to do work, even in an electric circuit. It is the energy that the charges carry that is ultimately responsible for causing a motor to spin to pump out your bilge, to start your engine, to ventilate your engine room, to hoist your dinghy aboard, or to pull your anchor out of the bottom. Electric energy has been converted to mechanical work in each case. At sunset, when you turn on your navigation lights, you see another type of energy conver-sion. The bulbs glow because their filaments have been heated to incandescence—electric energy has been converted to heat energy, and if the temperature is high enough, light energy will be emitted as well. Your depth sounder functions because electric energy is converted to sound energy by the transducer, a very special kind of crystal. In this case, the sound reflects off the bottom, returns and hits the crystal, which converts it back to the electric energy again. Yes, electric energy does work to perform many tasks for us on board.

## POWER

But *power* is a handier term to use than energy in describing the work of electrical devices. We define it this way:

---

*Power is the rate of doing work or expending energy.*

---

Symbolically, $P = W/T$. If one joule of energy is expended in one second, the power is one *watt*. One thousand watts is called a *kilowatt*, and 746 watts is equal to one *horsepower*. These terms are more familiar to us, I know. We buy lightbulbs by their wattage rating, we see kilowatt-hours every month on our electricity bill, and we use horsepower to rate the output of all kinds of engines, from lawn mowers to tugboat diesels. A 25-watt bulb can expend as much energy as a 100-watt bulb, but it will have to be lit four times as long. For the same time interval, the 100-watt bulb will use energy four times as fast as the 25-watt one. Leaving your 100-watt spreader lights on so you can find your boat after an evening of pub-crawling ashore will clobber your battery. We'll see why in a minute.

Power is also equal to the product of current times voltage. Using symbols we have already defined, $P = V \times I$ or in words,

---

*Watts equal volts times amps.*

---

This is one of the most useful formulas we have seen so far, but we more often use it to solve for the current I. Most all electrical devices will have their power rating indicated on the name plate—they hardly ever tell us what their current demand is. And we need that information in order to choose the proper size wire to hook up the device into a circuit. To get the current, just turn the formula around and solve for I = P/V, or,

---

*Amps equal watts divided by volts.*

---

Now let's look at those spreader lights you were going to leave on. They were 100 watts for the pair. For our 12-volt system, the current that has to flow in order to light them is equal to 100 watts divided by 12 volts, or 8.3 amps. You'll soon see this certainly is not an insignificant amount.

In order to simplify the arithmetic as much as possible, here is the first of our "Magic Triangles." It shows the relationship between power (P), current (I), and voltage (V), and tells us how to find an unknown value—just cover that one up, and the positions of the other two show the solution. Cover P; V and I are next to each other, multiply. Cover I; P is over V, divide.

Cover V; P is over I, divide. If my oversimplification offends some of you algebra scholars, I might remind you that several generations of U.S. armed forces electricians and electronic technicians learned their trade with the help of magic triangles, so don't knock it.

## AMP-HOURS

Closely related to current and power, especially for direct current systems that use a storage battery as the primary seat of EMF, is the concept of *amp-hours,* or the current multiplied by the time it flows. Amp-hours are used to describe a storage battery's *capacity;* how much charge it is capable of storing. It also is indicative of the rate at which a battery can be discharged, although that may be complicated by several other factors. Getting back to those spreader lights again—if you're gone for four hours, the amp-hours used will be 8.3 amps times 4 hours or 33 amp-hours. If you happen to get caught up in a singing contest someplace and stay an extra couple of hours, you may row home to find your spreader lights barely glowing a dull yellow. If that's your only battery, next morning you may find, in addition to the hangover, that the engine won't turn over. I always use a kerosene anchor light to avoid any prolonged drain on the battery. Even if the engine does crank and kick right off, you'll have to run it nearly three hours to get the battery fully recharged again. More about that later.

## RESISTANCE

The last term we have to define is *resistance*, which is the opposition to a current. For reasons that will soon be obvious, resistance is measured in units called *ohms*. While it acts something like friction, resistance actually is caused by the electrons colliding with atoms inside the wire and being slowed down and scattered. Even the best of conductors have some resistance. Others, such as light bulb filaments, have much more.

*Resistance always results in the conversion of electrical energy into heat.*

Except in the case of resistance heaters, it represents a waste of energy and an irretrievable loss to the system. The resistance of a wire depends upon three factors:

1. Type of metal (its resistivity)
2. Length of the wire
3. Cross-sectional area of the wire

Since practically all electrical wire is made of copper, we can ignore the first factor. Length of wire is always twice the distance between components—the current has to travel both "there" and "back." Whenever we talk about the "size" of a wire—always in American Wire Gauge or AWG numbers—we have to remember that large numbers are used for thin wires and small numbers for fat ones. If you ever have to replace or add some wiring on your boat, never use anything smaller than Number 16, and that only for low currents and short runs. We'll talk about how to make the actual selection later. Following our water analogy, it is easier for water to flow through a large pipe than it is through a very narrow one; the skinny pipe offers more water resistance. So small wires offer more resistance to the passage of an electrical current.

## ELECTRICITY IS NOT WATER, BUT . . .

Now that we have defined all the terms we need, here is a sketch of the complete water-analogy system, and also one of its electrical counterpart. We should be all done with the plumbing, now. From here on out, it's all electricity. In the next unit we'll describe each of the circuit components in greater detail.

**Figure 1–2**

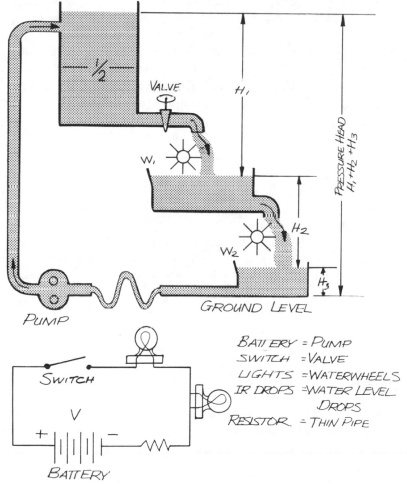

BATTERY = PUMP
SWITCH = VALVE
LIGHTS = WATERWHEELS
IR DROPS = WATER LEVEL DROPS
RESISTOR = THIN PIPE

## OHM'S LAW

In 1826 George Simon Ohm discovered the relationship between current, voltage, and resistance, which earned him his esteemed position as one of the founders of electrical science. At the time of his discovery, he was not only ignored, but was even fired from his high school teaching job. Only later, after others realized the fundamental importance of Ohm's Law, was he rescued from poverty and awarded a professorship at the University of Munich.

---

*Electric current is directly proportional to voltage and inversely proportional to resistance.*

---

That simple statement is Ohm's Law. Utterly simple and yet profound. Increase the voltage in a circuit and the current increases. Increase the resistance in a circuit and the current decreases. In symbols it's $I = V/R$ and $R = V/I$ and $V = I \times R$.

All three equations say the same thing, it just depends on which variable you need to find. This sketch of Ohm's Triangle makes it easy to do the calculations without having to remember all the formulas. The triangle has three boxes, V, I, and R. Just cover up the one you want to find, and do the arithmetic that is indicated. If you want V, cover it and I and R are next to each other; multiply. If you want I, cover it and V is over R; divide. If you want R, cover it and V is over I; divide. If a voltage of one volt is impressed on a circuit whose resistance is one ohm, then one amp of current will flow.

## IR DROPS AND I²R HEAT

A few pages back when we were talking about the rule of electricity which says the EMF of the source is equal to the voltage drops around a circuit—known as *Kirchoff's Law* in physics books—we were referring to the third form of Ohm's equation, $V = I \times R$. In every item that offers resistance, the voltage drop across it is equal to the current through it times the resistance. We commonly refer to these effects as *IR drops*. The loss of energy by having it converted to heat in a resistance is always expressed in terms of power rather than energy. Remember that $P = V \times I$, and since $V = I \times R$, then $P = (I \times R) \times I$ or $P = I \times I \times R$ or $P = I^2 R$. Heat losses are always referred to as *$I^2 R$ losses;* spoken "I squared R."

In our home kitchen, not likely our galley, we have several electric devices that we want to heat, such as a toaster and a light bulb. The toaster will dissipate about 1,200 watts, the light bulb 100. Let's see how they work on 120 volts (don't worry whether it is AC or DC) by calculating the current through each, and then the resistance of each.

> TOASTER:
> $I = P/V = 1200$ watts/120 volts $= 10$ amps
> and $R = V/I = 120$ volts/10 amps $= 12$ ohms

> LIGHT BULB:
> $I = P/V = 100$ watts/120 volts $= 0.83$ amps
> $R = V/I = 120$ volts/0.83 amps $= 144$ ohms

The resistance of the light bulb is 12 times that of the toaster. What this means is that to toast bread you need lots of heat power. Since heat power is $I^2R$, you need a large current, which is obtained by using a lower resistance. In the light bulb, only the tiny filament needs to be heated to give off light. Not much current is needed, so the resistance is considerably larger.

If all this is new to you, you may want to reread this section. It is important to lay these foundations early. We'll be calling on them again. But the math won't get any harder.

## CHAPTER 2

# ELECTRIC CIRCUITS

## Parts Of The System

### CIRCUIT COMPONENTS

Back in the last chapter, the water system analogy was an example of a simple complete electric circuit. Now we want to take a closer look at circuits in general in order to see what parts are needed to make them up, how the parts are hooked together, and how they operate. Eventually you'll want to be able to diagram your own electrical system. It'll help you when you want to make changes to your system and when you need to isolate problems.

First let's look at some of the standard symbols that are used in circuit diagrams to represent the various elements of the actual electric circuit.

**SOURCE** may be a CELL ⊥⊢ or a BATTERY ⊥|ı|ı|⊢ Each set (a long thin line and a short thick line) is a cell. The thin line is the positive end and the thick one is negative. A battery consists of *two or more cells*. A flashlight battery really consists of all the cells in it. But if you ask the store clerk for a flashlight cell, he probably won't know what you're talking about. Most everyone uses these terms incorrectly. Now in most 12-volt

boat or car batteries there actually are 6 cells; each is physically separated from its neighbor cells, but electrically interconnected, and each has its own filler hole for adding
water and checking the specific gravity of the electrolyte,
unless it's one of the new "maintenance free" batteries—
more about them later.

The source may also be a GENERATOR $\textcircled{G}$ or ALTER-
NATOR $\textcircled{A}$ or an AC PLUG $\equiv\!\!\!D\!\!=$ connected to a
rectifier. The circuit doesn't really care what is supplying
the EMF. In addition to these more or less standard types
of sources you might also add as an optional or auxiliary
source a photovoltaic solar cell panel to convert solar energy directly into electricity, a wind generator to convert
the wind's energy into electricity, either while at anchor or
underway, or a water-powered generator to produce electricity from the boat's motion through the water. None of
these latter sources are stock items on factory-built boats.
If you want to add one, you'll have to buy it and then install
it yourself or have it installed.

**CONDUCTOR** or wire is a solid line——. The special
solid conductors found inside a control panel box to which
all appliance connections are made are called **BUS BARS**.
They are usually strips of copper, drilled and tapped for
attaching screws.

**JUNCTION** of conductors, or conductor and some other
unit, is shown by a dot on the intersection, like a drop of
solder to seal the connection. Conductors crossing without
being electrically connected are shown without the dot or
with a bulge indicating a "bridge" crossover. All boat wiring is of the "two-wire" type, a "hot" wire ultimately con-
nects the unit to the positive terminal of the source and a
"return" wire leads back to the negative terminal. Both are
insulated and must be of the same size. This is different
from automobile 12-volt DC wiring which usually uses
only a single "hot" wire to each electrical component; the

metal in the car body and chassis is used for the "return" path back to the source.

**RESISTOR** (Symbol R) or **LOAD** is a zigzag line ─/\/\─ , which is reminiscent of the way resistors were made in the early days of electrical science—a length of resistance wire was folded back and forth many times.

**SWITCH** (S) is the device used to control the circuit. The symbol looks just like the old knife-blade ─•⁄•─ hinged connectors used to " close," "make," "complete," or "turn on" the circuit when desired, and to "open," "break," "disconnect," or "turn it off" when finished.

**FUSE** (F) is an automatic safety switch incorporated ─•∿•─ into a circuit to protect it from overload. A commonly used type consists of a glass tube containing a short piece of wire of low melting point. When the current in the circuit exceeds the amperage rating of the fuse, the wire melts and breaks the circuit, the same as if the switch were opened. This is because of the $I^2 R$ heating effect of a current, which we learned about in the last chapter.

**CIRCUIT BREAKER** is another type of automatic safety switch which performs the same function as a fuse; it breaks the circuit in case of overload. The circuit breaker is actuated either magnetically or thermally, and it can be reset merely by throwing a switch instead of being replaced. We'll see more about them later.

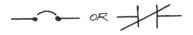

**COIL** is a tube of wire wound round and round. We don't have much use for coils in DC electricity, except in the ignition system of a gasoline engine, or as part of some other device such as a RELAY or TRANSFORMER. The "solenoid" that makes the circuit in the engine starter when you press the starter button, is actually a relay, or remotely controlled switch, as we will see later. Its coil portion is usually sketched as ‾𝟘𝟘𝟘𝟘𝟘𝟘𝟘‾

**A TRANSFORMER** consists of two coils, the PRIMARY and the SECONDARY, which are magnetically coupled together with an iron core. When oscillating or pulsating electrical energy is fed into the primary at one voltage, then the secondary coil produces alternating electrical energy (AC), usually at a different voltage. If the secondary coil has many more turns or loops of wire in it than the primary coil, the transformer is said to be a "step-up" transformer. It will deliver more AC voltage than was present in the primary circuit. The ignition coil on any gasoline engine is a good example of a "step-up" transformer. The 12 volts in the primary circuit are "stepped-up" or multiplied to several tens of thousands of volts in the secondary for delivery to the spark plugs. On the other hand, if the secondary coil has *fewer* turns in it than the primary coil, then the device is called a "step-down" transformer; the secondary will deliver *less* voltage than is present in the primary. If you use a battery charger aboard, plugged into shore power AC, the transformer will reduce the voltage from 120 volts to 12 volts, and then a rectifier will convert the AC to DC. We'll learn more about these later, too. If this brief discussion about transformers leads you to suspect that you can get something for nothing—forget it. You *can* increase the voltage with a step-up transformer, but only at the expense of the current. Remember that power is equal to amps times volts ($P = I \times V$), and the power of the secondary is equal to the power of the primary, except for slight losses in the device itself. If you step-up the volts, the amps must decrease proportionally; no free lunch here.

**GROUND** refers to a connection made to the earth itself. The symbol is made up of several parallel lines of diminishing lengths. The English call it "earth," rather than "ground." On land, a ground connection is made to a rod or pipe driven several feet into the ground. On our boats, the connection is ultimately made to seawater, often through the engine, shaft, and propeller, or to a separate ground plate, or to the ballast keel, if external. The American Boat and Yacht Council recommends the negative ground system in which the negative leg of the battery circuit is connected directly to the boat's engine as the common ground. Each item in the circuit is connected by its own pair of wires and the common ground carries no load current. If you discover that your boat is NOT wired in this way, I highly recommend that you look up the April 1984 issue of *Cruising World* and read Robert Merriam's "Exposing the Myth of 'The Great Floating Ground'" to find out why it should be changed to comply. Ground is considered to be either an infinite "sink" or an infinite "source" for charge. That means if we have an excess of charge, ground will take all we can give it. If we have a deficiency of charge, ground will supply us with all we need.

**TRANSDUCER** is the term used for a device that exchanges one kind of energy for another. We already talked about the depth sounder transducer in the last chapter. A light bulb is a transducer that changes electrical energy into light energy, plus heat as an unwanted byproduct. A horn changes electrical energy into sound energy. A motor changes electrical energy into mechanical energy. A radio changes electrical energy into electromagnetic radiation while transmitting, and electromagnetic radiations into sound while receiving. And so on. The transducer is the reason we put electricity aboard our boats in the first place. If it didn't do useful work, we wouldn't need it, would we?

An **INVERTER** is a device sometimes used on a boat to change the boat's 12-volt DC into household voltage (120-

volt) AC so that some "home" appliances can be used aboard. They are usually not used on a boat with limited battery capacity. The conversion is always less than 100% efficient, even with solid-state devices, and the AC produced is not the same as found in home wiring (for the technically-minded, it is "square wave" AC rather than "sine wave" AC). Those appliances that operate because of resistance heating (coffee makers, toasters, etc.) don't know the difference, and TV's, stereos, and most hand tools will work OK on inverter output. But capacitor and split-phase motor appliances—like refrigerators and air conditioners— won't work. So check it out before you buy and install one. Some low-wattage inverters are fairly inexpensive, a 200-watt inverter can be found for under $100. But high-demand inverters can be quite costly. If you find you need a lot of AC aboard, I'd look for another way of getting it.

We have just listed practically all the circuit components you might expect to find on board your boat. What is the minimum needed to make a circuit? Well, if you remember back in the Preface, we spoke about inadvertently dropping a wrench or screwdriver onto both battery terminals. That makes a complete circuit; rather spectacular, but not very useful. The minimum useful circuit should have 4 components:

1. A source to maintain the potential difference and supply energy to the charges
2. A transducer to do the useful work (the "load")
3. A switch to control the circuit
4. Conductors or wires to hook them all together

Remember this is the *minimum* requirement for a useful circuit. There may be several other components in the same circuit, and they may be hooked up in several different ways. The very simple circuits are not unusual on our boats, though. Every circuit you have aboard that contains only one item is just this simple. The list usually includes your depth sounder circuit, your radio circuit, your horn circuit, and on a sailboat your masthead light (or steaming light) circuit.

The circuits for navigation lights and cabin lights both contain several different lights; the navigation lights all come on together when the switch is thrown—except for sailboats which must use the masthead light only while under power, never under sail alone. The cabin lights may or may not all work together; usually each is independent of the others with its own switch, but they are all part of the same circuit. Multiple-unit circuits are more complicated to work than the simple ones with only a single function, for obvious reasons. When you have trouble, there are more places to look to find the cause.

## SERIES CIRCUITS

A series circuit is one in which the current has to pass through each and every component of the circuit, one after the other. The same amount of current is found in all the component parts—wires, transducers and source. If there is an interruption or break in the circuit at any place, the current stops. The old-fashioned Christmas tree light strings were always connected in series, but not too many people still remember them—and for good reason. Whenever one bulb burned out, they all quit. Then you had to unscrew and test each bulb until you finally found the bad one, and then replace it. No wonder parallel-wired lights took over the Christmas tree market. But let's not get ahead of ourselves.

Here is a simple series circuit drawn in schematic form with

**Figure 2–1:** *Series circuit*

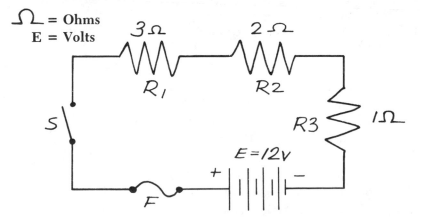

some assumed values shown so we can go through the basic calculations which are necessary to analyze it.

In analyzing circuits, we usually assume that the resistance of the wires is negligible compared with the other resistances present in the circuit. But we know that all conductors have *some* resistance, so for long runs of small diameter wire, this assumption may not be valid, and we will have to allow for wire voltage drop when we select a wire size to use. We'll ignore it for now, but come back to it later. Notice that our circuit, as drawn, is incomplete or open. No current will flow until the switch is closed. The source is maintaining 12 volts of potential difference between the ends of the circuit, but no electrons are moving yet.

How much current will be in the circuit when the switch is closed? We can calculate that ahead of time by adding up all the resistance present.

---

*For a series circuit, the total resistance of the circuit is equal to the sum of all the individual resistances.*

---

In an equation it's shown as: $R_T = R_1 + R_2 + R_3 + \ldots R_n$. In this circuit there are three resistances, $R_1 = 3$ ohms, $R_2 = 2$ ohms, and $R_3 = 1$ ohm. The abbreviation for ohm is the Greek letter omega, which looks like a horseshoe, $\Omega$. So the total circuit resistance is $3 + 2 + 1 = 6$ ohms.

Now we go back to Ohm's Triangle. We know the voltage is 12 volts, and the circuit resistance is 6 ohms. Current I, is unknown, but must be equal to $V/R_T$ or 12 volts/6 ohms = 2 amps. So when the switch is closed, 2 amps of current will pass through the fuse, through the switch, through each of the resistors and wires and through the battery. That is the nature of the simple series circuit. If we have only one transducer, resistor, or load in a circuit, it is a series circuit. Its hookup, analysis and possible repair are relatively simple.

Before we leave the series circuit, let's check it out with Kirchoff's Law. Is the EMF of the source really equal to the sum of the IR drops around the circuit? E = 12 volts. I = 2 amps for each resistor, so

$$E = IR_1 + IR_2 + IR_3$$

12 volts = 2 amps × 3 ohms + 2 amps × 2 ohms + 2 amps × 1 ohm

12 volts = 6 volts + 4 volts + 2 volts

12 volts = 12 volts, sure enough.

What about the power consumed in a series circuit? For each load, power equals voltage times current or P = V × I.

$P_1$ = 6 volts × 2 amps =    12 watts
$P_2$ = 4 volts × 2 amps =     8 watts
$P_3$ = 2 volts × 2 amps =     4 watts
Sum of the three powers = 24 watts

Total power equals $I^2R_T$ = $2^2$ × 6 ohms = 4 × 6 = 24 watts. Comes out the same both ways, must be right.

That should satisfy our curiosity about series circuits, now let's look at some more complicated ones, but not too complicated.

## PARALLEL CIRCUITS

The identifying characteristic of parallel circuits is the presence of *branch points*, which are points where the current can split up or divide. The same current does not have to flow through each and every component of the circuit. There are alternate paths for the current to follow, but in each case the amount of current in that path is inversely proportional to the resistance of the branch—the higher the resistance, the less current the path will use. Also, all the individual currents that have split up at one branch point must all come together at another branch point. Current cannot accumulate in any part of the circuit. Kirchoff gave us another of his Laws, this one about current for parallel circuits, which says:

*At any junction of conductors, the algebraic sum of the currents is zero.*

This just means what goes in must come out. If we call "going in" positive and "coming out" negative, then the pluses and minuses must be equal and add up to zero.

Every circuit with more than one transducer in it, such as our cabin lights circuit, or our navigation lights circuit, will be a parallel circuit. Often we may use an existing circuit to tie in a new piece of electrical gear; we'll be adding it in parallel to the existing component, so we must have an understanding of what that will do to the circuit so we can tell whether the modification is safe or not. Those new-style Christmas tree lights reveal the true advantage of the parallel circuit over the series circuit. When a bulb burns out its filament breaks and it stops glowing, but all the rest of the circuit stays lit. The bad bulb has no apparent effect on the others—they keep on glowing. It's easy to find the bad one to change it.

The one factor that is common to a parallel group of resistors or loads is the voltage across them, so each resistor will have the same IR drop. This next sentence may sound strange at first, but here goes. The more branch paths or resistors that are added in parallel, the less total opposition there is to the flow of current.

---

*If we add resistors in parallel the total resistance goes down.*

---

Not only goes down, but the new total resistance is LESS than the SMALLEST single resistor. Think about that. That's why I said we really have to understand what happens when we add a new component to an existing circuit. If we merely jump it across a nearby lamp outlet, without planning ahead or doing any calculations, we may completely overload that circuit —with resulting chronic fuseblowing problems or popping circuit breakers or even a possible fire hazard if the circuit is unprotected.

Here is what a simple parallel circuit looks like. We'll use the same size resistors as we did in the series circuit, only connect them in parallel with each other. That way we can better compare the results of the two different hookups. I show a circuit switch, such as would be in your control panel, as well as individual switches for each load, so you can use only the ones actually needed. The battery EMF is still 12 volts, and the circuit is fuse protected. Points A and B are the branch points. The currents that were divided at "A" must later come together at "B."

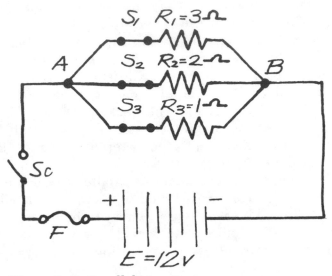

**Figure 2–2:** *Parallel circuit*

In order to begin our analysis of the parallel circuit, we must first determine the total circuit resistance.

---

*The reciprocal of the total circuit resistance of a parallel circuit is equal to the sum of the reciprocals of all the individual branch resistances.*

---

The reciprocal is just one divided by the number, i.e., the reciprocal of A is 1/A, the reciprocal of R is 1/R. So the equation for parallel resistors (let's say there are "n" of them) is: $1/R_T = 1/R_1 + 1/R_2 + 1/R_3 \ldots 1/R_n$. It does look different from the series equation. Here's how to use it. In our sketch: $1/R_T = 1/3 + 1/2 + 1/1$. Use a common denominator of 6, or do each fraction on your calculator separately. Thus, $1/R_T = 2/6 + 3/6 + 6/6 = 11/6$. Then $R_T = 6/11$ or 0.545 ohms.

The total resistance of these three resistors connected in parallel is just a little more than one-half ohm. When connected in series, the total resistance was 6 ohms. When the circuit switch is closed, how much current, $I_C$, will flow through the fuse, switch and battery? We go back to Ohm's Law again, with V = 12 volts, and $R_T$ = 0.545 ohms. So, $I_C$ = $V/R_T$ = 22 amps! Now that's a LOT of current. Can that be right? Let's check the voltage drop across points A and B; it must be the same as the battery voltage: 22 amps × 0.545 ohms = 12 volts. Must be correct. Now let's look at the current through each limb of the parallel arrangement.

$$\text{In } R_1 , I_1 = 12 \text{ volts/3 ohms} = 4 \text{ amps}$$
$$\text{In } R_2 , I_1 = 12 \text{ volts/2 ohms} = 6 \text{ amps}$$
$$\text{In } R_3 , I_3 = 12 \text{ volts/1 ohm} = 12 \text{ amps}$$

So the total current is 4 + 6 + 12 = 22 amps. It splits up three ways at A and then all comes back together at B. The sum of these three currents is the same as that in the main circuit. So Kirchoff's Current Law must be correct; what comes in must go out.

The only thing left to check on is the power consumption in the parallel circuit and its branches. P = V × I = $I^2R$

$$\text{For } P_1 = 12 \text{ volts} × 4 \text{ amps} = 48 \text{ watts}$$
$$P_2 = 12 \text{ volts} = 6 \text{ amps} = 72 \text{ watts}$$
$$P_3 = 12 \text{ volts} × 12 \text{ amps} = 144 \text{ watts}$$
$$\text{Sum of the three powers} = 264 \text{ watts}$$
$$\text{Circuit power} = I^2R_T = (22)^2 × 0.545 = 264 \text{ watts}$$

Now go back and look at each of these figures: total resistance, voltage drops, and power consumption for the series circuit with the same resistors. Side by side comparison will make the differences all the more apparent. The very same circuit components, hooked up differently, can give vastly different performance characteristics.

I have over-simplified a few things in this discussion, but have done so on purpose, to avoid becoming bogged down in minor points. I have omitted any discussion of battery resistance here—we'll get to that in a later section when we look at recharging the battery.

## CHAPTER 3

# THE BATTERY

## Heart Of The System

### PRIMARY AND SECONDARY CELLS

A voltaic cell is any device in which chemical reactions are used to supply electrical energy. The cell is a basic unit, just like in a jail or a monastery. But a group of those small rooms is called a cell-block; a group of voltaic cells is called a battery. Things may not always be as they seem, as I try to illustrate in the photo, Figure 3-1.

**Figure 3–1:** *Dry cells and a battery*

The top row are all cells, commonly called "dry cells," which we have used all our lives for various electrical devices—flashlights, calculators, portable radios, RDFs, and so on. The sizes shown are AA, C, and D, all 1.5-volt types. All are called primary cells, which means that they are throwaways. As we use them, some of the material that makes them up is consumed. Eventually, when they become "weak" due to depletion of the material to the point where the chemical reaction will no longer continue, they have to be replaced. And they are not dry at all. If you have ever left some cells in an electronic device for several years, when you finally opened it up again you may have seen a gooey mess all over everything, ruining your flashlight or radio. Cells that get dim after continuous use may bounce back and work fine the next day for a while. They didn't heal themselves miraculously; what happened is called depolarization. Gases are generated in the cell during operation. These gases may collect on the electrodes and interfere with their performance. Letting the cells rest allows the gases to be removed by some secondary chemical reactions. The cell will then give normal current for a short time until polarization starts again. The useful intervals get shorter and shorter as the end approaches.

The familiar 9-volt transistor battery is shown on the second row of the photo. I opened up an old one to show you that the proper word this time is "battery." Six individual cells are built into the small rectangular steel box as you can see. All are connected in series, so the total voltage is $6 \times 1.5 = 9$ volts. Six-volt lantern batteries have four cells inside them, and 12-volt batteries have 8.

In most electronic stores and discount department stores you can find inexpensive so-called battery "chargers" for allegedly recharging various size primary cells. If you read the literature carefully, you'll see they say "revitalize" or "rejuvenate" your batteries. Primary cells can't be recharged, but their performance can be improved for a while. If your kids have some toys or games that gobble up dry cells, sure it's a good investment. But for only occasional use, I doubt that they're worthwhile having. It'll take a long time to pay back the initial investment.

However, cells made from nickel and cadmium, called "Ni-Cads," are rechargeable. Their reaction is electrically and chemically reversible. It's not a good idea to use alkaline or carbon batteries in chargers designed for nickel-cadmium batteries, because they can explode. All this leads us into the topic of SECONDARY CELLS. A secondary cell is one that is reversible in that the material consumed in producing electricity can be regenerated to its original form by passing an electric current through it in the opposite direction. If several of these cells are joined together in a single unit, it is called a storage battery. Now that is important to us on our boat, so let's get right to it.

## PURPOSE AND FUNCTION OF THE STORAGE BATTERY

In the anatomy of your boat's electrical system, the storage battery is the heart. It pumps the electrons through the wires that make up the various circuits. The battery is an electrochemical device; it stores chemical energy that can be converted to electrical energy. A chemical reaction inside the battery cells maintains a potential difference or voltage between the positive and negative terminals, which "pumps" or pushes electrons around whichever circuits are closed or completed. No charges should flow through an open or incomplete circuit; but sometimes they do, though. When that happens, you've got a problem—which we'll get to in the troubleshooting section. Whenever a switch is thrown connecting the battery to an external load, such as the starter, navigation lights, radio, loran, or satnav, chemical energy is converted to electrical energy and a current flows through the circuit.

The storage battery's chemical reaction is reversible, which means that it can be recharged, and will be, continuously, as long as the engine is running and the alternator or generator is functioning properly, or one of the auxiliary charging devices —solar, wind, or water driven, is in operation. Normally, we take these things for granted, and are surprised when they don't work—a testament to the reliability of the devices.

In your boat, as in your car or truck, the battery serves three main functions, as explained by the Battery Council International in its "Battery Service Manual":

1. It supplies power to the starter and (on gasoline engines) the ignition system.
2. It supplies the extra power needed when the total electrical load exceeds the amount being generated.
3. It acts like a shock absorber or voltage stabilizer for the whole electrical system. It reduces or smooths out temporarily high voltages (transients), which could cause damage to sensitive electronic components.

The complete chemistry of storage battery reactions is complex, but let's simplify it as much as possible, so we understand how it works, to know how best to maintain it. Most boat batteries in use are of the 12-volt lead-acid type, the same generic type used in most motor vehicles. Unfortunately, many of these boat batteries are the *same* as car batteries, often masquerading as boat batteries. Just because somebody slaps on a sticker that says "Marine" and gives it a salty-looking rope carry strap, doesn't make it a true boat battery. Admitting that you use the battery on a boat just cuts the warranty period in half, or less, and raises the price. We'll discuss the characteristics of a good marine battery as we go along.

All lead-acid batteries contain the same chemical ingredients, and undergo the same chemical reactions. Here's what they're made of:

1. Sponge Lead (Pb). This material makes up the negative plates in all of the cells. It is metallic lead.
2. Lead dioxide ($Pb\ O_2$). The material on all the positive plates in the cells.
3. Sulfuric acid ($H_2\ SO_4$). The electrolyte or liquid in the cells.

Whenever two dissimilar metals are immersed in an electrolyte, a voltage develops between them. One of the metals tries to give away electrons so it can go into solution in the electrolyte as an ion, becoming the negative terminal. The other metal becomes the positive electrode. Stick a piece of copper and a piece of zinc into a pickle or an olive, and you can measure the voltage between the metals with a voltmeter. In this case the brine is the electrolyte, copper and zinc are the dissimilar metals; zinc becomes the negative electrode and copper the positive. The actual voltage depends on the types of metals used and the electrolyte. When I did this experiment in my kitchen with some ingredients out of the refrigerator and a pair of copper and zinc strips, I got the following results:

Green Olive with Pimento     0.6 volts, 0.1 ma initial current
Wife's Homemade Dill Pickle    0.8 volts, 0.5 ma initial current

Let's see now, 15 pickles in series should give 12 volts. Hmmm . . .

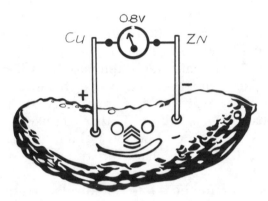

*"All right, you pickles, line up in a single file, end to end! If we all get together, maybe we can solve this energy problem everybody's talking about."*

For a lead—acid battery, the potential is approximately 2.1 volts per cell. As soon as one of the switches is thrown to complete a circuit the chemical reactions start and electrical energy flows from the battery, carried by electrons moving through the external circuit, and as ions inside the battery, between the plates.

## WHAT HAPPENS WHEN DISCHARGING

The discharge cycle begins just as soon as current starts to flow from a battery through an external load. The positive plates are made from a compound of lead (Pb) and oxygen (O) —lead dioxide (Pb $O_2$). The electrolyte consists of sulfuric acid ($H_2 SO_4$), which is a compound of hydrogen (H) and sulfate ion ($SO_4$). The negative plates are made of lead metal, spongy in texture. As discharge continues, some of the lead in the positive plate combines with sulfate from the electrolyte to form lead sulfate ($PbSO_4$) on the positive plates. Oxygen in these same positive plates combines with hydrogen from the sulfuric acid to form water ($H_2O$), which then reduces the acid solution concentration and thus lowers its specific gravity.

Over on the negative plates, the same reaction is occuring. Lead (spongy type) is combining with sulfate ions from the acid to form lead sulfate ($PbSO_4$). Now remember, we said the thing that makes a cell work was the two dissimilar metals in an electrolyte. But now both these plates, dissimilar at first, are turning into the same stuff, lead sulfate. The more alike they become, the less is the cell voltage. And the electrolyte is becoming more diluted with water and thus weaker. Eventually, when it can no longer deliver energy at a useful voltage, the battery will become discharged.

Cranking a hard-to-start engine on a cold day will discharge a battery in just a few minutes. Did you ever wonder why? Of course the thicker oil in the crankcase makes it harder for the starter to turn the engine over, but the reason for quick discharge lies within the battery. Here, for the first time, we see the fundamental difference between a battery built for starting engines and one built for lower discharge rates. On cold starting, where starter currents can be in the hundreds of amperes, a lot of chemical reaction is needed. But the acid can only react with the lead metal it can touch. A solid smooth sheet of metal would allow the acid to contact only the molecules on the outside. But since starting batteries need a large surface contact area, porous, low-density material, with lots of nooks and crannies, allows deep penetration by the acid solution, and so is used to make their plates. Even so, on cold days acid circulation and diffusion of the newly-formed water molecules out of the pores proceeds very slowly. That's why your battery dies so quickly when you crank and crank on a cold day—and, also, why, if you let it rest for 15 or 20 minutes it will bounce right back.

A battery not primarily used for starting does not need so much surface area of plate material. The rate of reaction is slower when all you need is a few amps for a set of running lights while under sail. Even in cold weather, this type battery will not be limited by poor acid circulation and water diffusion. But it may become nearly completely discharged by a low load for a long time; which could consume practically all the acid.

This type of battery is known as a "house" or "ship" battery. Instead of porous plates, it needs THICK ones. Because house batteries may be nearly discharged and then recharged many times over their lifetime, they are called "deep-cycle" batteries. Completely run down your auto-type battery 20 or 30 times, and it'll be ready for the scrap man to melt down into some new ballast. Good heavy-duty, deep-cycle batteries will withstand hundreds of discharge-charge cycles. But nothing lasts forever; eventually the plates or separator will deteriorate and ultimately the battery will fail. You know you'll have to pay for this superior performance. You won't find heavy-duty, deep-cycle batteries in the discount chain department stores or at your corner service station.

## WHAT HAPPENS WHEN CHARGING

When the battery is charging, the current is passed through it in the opposite direction as during discharge, restoring the active chemicals to their initial condition. The lead sulfate ($PbSO_4$) that was formed on both plates is broken up into Pb and $SO_4$. All of these fragments start out as ions, carrying + or − charges, but for simplicity we are ignoring this stage of the game. The water dissociates into hydrogen 2 (H) and oxygen (O). Now the sulfate can combine with the hydrogen to re-form sulfuric acid ($H_2SO_4$), while the oxygen combines with lead to form lead dioxide ($PbO_2$). The sulfuric acid that is forming is more dense than the water that is disappearing, so the specific gravity (defined in the next section) of the electrolyte is increasing.

What causes a charging battery to bubble and gurgle as it nears full charge? The bubbles are the hydrogen and oxygen gases. Hydrogen is given off at the negative plate and oxygen at the positive plate; both come from water being decomposed, and together they form a HIGHLY EXPLOSIVE MIXTURE. Gassing is a sign that the charging rate is greater than the battery can handle. Several factors may be causing gassing:

1. The battery is fully charged already.
2. The battery plates are sulfated.
3. The battery is too cold to take the charge.

Gassing usually occurs near the end of the charge cycle. It can be reduced by using a charger or regulator that reduces the charge rate as the battery nears the full-charge condition. Sealed, low-maintenance batteries must not be overcharged and gassed-out because there is no way to replace the water when lost.

## ELECTROLYTE AND HYDROMETERS

As we have said, battery electrolyte is a sulfuric acid solution. But it is not all acid. It is only 25% acid by volume and 75% water. Acid should never be added to the battery; add only water. What kind? Distilled water is best. You don't have to buy distilled water for the battery. You can get pure water from your dehumidifier or from your freezer when you defrost it. Actually, you can use any water fit to drink, as long as the mineral content is not too high. But since we don't always know how high it is, distilled water is a better choice.

Specific gravity is a measure of the relative heaviness of anything, compared with pure water. Water has a specific gravity of 1. A fully-charged battery's electrolyte will have a specific gravity of 1.265 when corrected to 80 degrees F; it will weigh 1.265 times as much as pure water. Specific gravity can be measured with a hydrometer; an instrument consisting of a glass or plastic tube with a calibrated float inside, a squeeze bulb on one end and a hose on the other to suck up electrolyte. The more dense the electrolyte, the higher the float will ride, and the higher the specific gravity reading. Discharging depletes the acid content, and builds up the water, so a low specific gravity indicates a run-down battery. A reading of 1.160 indicates only ¼ charge remaining.

Figure 3-2 shows two different hydrometers found in most auto stores. The smaller sells for less than a dollar, but is not as accurate as the other. Four little weighted balls float to indicate the state of charge of the battery; each stands for ¼ charge. When all 4 float, it's fully charged. When none float, it's flat-out dead. But small bubbles can stick to the balls and give erroneously high readings. The balls sometimes hang up until you shake them loose, and acid will eventually reduce the transpar-

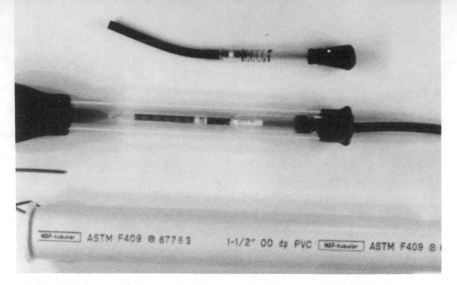

**Figure 3–2:** *Two inexpensive battery hydrometers and a PVC holster for stowing the larger model.*

ency of the tube. I have had one aboard for several years, so I know its shortcomings. It is easy to stow, and the price is surely right. The larger hydrometer sells for around three dollars. It has a glass tube and a calibrated float that gives actual specific gravity readings. If you buy one, make sure you get the battery model, and not the one for anti-freeze!! They look identical, except for the float. I keep mine in a PVC holster, as shown. The wire hook lets me hang it out of the way where it won't get broken. On this model (Rex Automotive) the float is color-coded:

```
                1.100
RED                      DISCHARGED CONDITION
————→   1.225   ←————
WHITE                    NEEDS ATTENTION
————→   1.260   ←————
GREEN                    O.K.
                1.300
```

The specific gravity reading is taken at the liquid level when the hydrometer is held at eye height. Be very careful of your eyes when using a hydrometer. Wear protective glasses or an eye shield. Temperature has a considerable influence on both specific gravity and battery operation, as we have already seen. The hydrometer floats are calibrated at 80 degrees F (26.7° C), so whenever the temperature deviates from that value, a correction should be applied to the reading. The following table shows how to do that. When the temperature is above 80° F, the reading is too low, so you have to add a little to it; when it's below 80° F the reading is too high, so you have to subtract the correction, which is .004 for each 10° F (or 5.5° C).

## PREVENTING FREEZING

If you happen to be lucky enough to live where water never freezes, you'll find that batteries are prepared with a specific gravity of 1.225 for fully charged, and 1.115 for 25% of charge. This will add to battery life because the plates and separators

Figure 3–3: *Temperature corrections for hydrometer readings. (Courtesy of Battery Council International, Chicago.)*

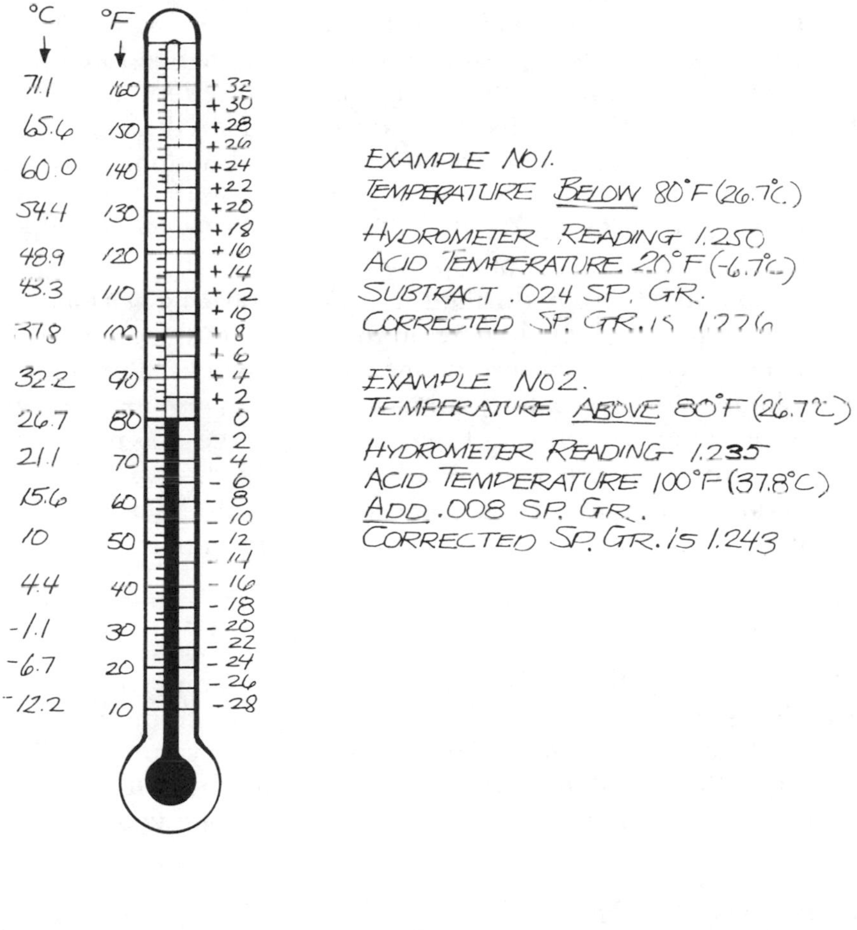

EXAMPLE NO 1.
TEMPERATURE BELOW 80°F (26.7°C)

HYDROMETER READING 1.250
ACID TEMPERATURE 20°F (-6.7°C)
SUBTRACT .024 SP. GR.
CORRECTED SP. GR. IS 1.226

EXAMPLE NO 2.
TEMPERATURE ABOVE 80°F (26.7°C)

HYDROMETER READING 1.235
ACID TEMPERATURE 100°F (37.8°C)
ADD .008 SP. GR.
CORRECTED SP. GR. IS 1.243

won't deteriorate so quickly. Your cold-cranking performance also will diminish, but you don't need it if it's not so cold. In extremely cold climates, a stronger electrolyte will be used to give the necessary cold-cranking oomph—up to a maximum of 1.300. Any more than that will decrease the service life of the battery.

Can batteries freeze? They sure can, if they're run down. At a specific gravity of 1.120, which is considered to be completely discharged, the electrolyte will freeze at $+14°$ F. But when fully charged at 1.260, the freezing point is lowered to $-73°$ F! If you stay down in the Florida Keys, don't worry about it. But if you're in New England or the Great Lakes, you get the idea of what will happen if you forget to remove the battery when you lay up your vessel for the winter season. Not only that, but there's another twist to the story. Automobile batteries have an inadvertent built-in discharge mechanism. In order to increase the strength of the grid, which is the backbone or skeleton of the plates, lead is alloyed with antimony (maintenance-free batteries now use calcium for this, and avoid the problem). During charging, some antimony dissolves and ends up on the negative plates' sponge lead, where it sets up a "local action," like a short circuit, which can eventually discharge the negative plates. According to the Battery Council International, the charge-loss rate averages out to about .001 specific gravity or "gravity points" per day during the summer boating season. It is less in winter, and much more on really hot days. Leave your boat unattended on its mooring for five or six weeks, and you'll likely find a sluggish battery upon return. Leave your battery aboard over the winter and it may self-discharge down to the point where it can freeze, possibly rupturing the case. Then you've got a bilge full of acid in addition to a defunct battery. Routine maintenance and inspection really are important.

## USING A HYDROMETER

Before leaving the hydrometer, here are a couple of nitty-gritty hints about using one. The acid withdrawn from one cell should always be returned to the same cell after you make the reading. If the liquid level is too low, you won't be able to suck up any acid. You'll have to add water first. But then you'll have to charge the battery before you can get a valid reading from that cell. If you check too soon, you'll get a value that's too low. The charging will increase the specific gravity, of course, but the low-density fresh water you just added will lie on the top until gassing begins, which will stir up and mix the acid and water. If that same cell is habitually low, you'll soon be needing a new battery. If the battery was near complete discharge, it may require many hours before it is fully recharged. If you check a battery too soon after heavy cranking, the new water formed will not have had time to get out of the plates and mix, so the value will be too high.

## STORAGE BATTERY CONSTRUCTION

Most of us have never seen the inside of a battery. In fact, we seldom even see pictures of what is in there—six holes for water and a couple of terminals to hook it up with and the rest is a mystery. I hope these illustrations will help to reduce that mystery.

## DIFFERENTIATING BETWEEN BATTERIES

All batteries look about the same at a distance. Automotive, commercial and marine batteries all have the same basic components, but each is engineered for its own specific tasks and is built to survive in its own environment. If there is one single criterion for judging how good a new battery is, I would pick weight. Weight usually indicates two things: more plate material and a stronger case—both will lead to longer battery life on your boat. Even if you use an auto battery on board, get the heaviest one. Check the specs in a catalog, such as Sears. I have never had an electric starter on board. I hand crank my Sabb diesel on *Integrity,* so our electrical demands are quite low, even when living aboard for up to a year at a time. I have always been able to get by with an auto battery. But I buy the largest and heaviest one with the longest warranty that will fit into one of our cars. When you carefully check the spec sheet and price list, you'll find that many stores charge the same price for all batteries of the same category—all 48-month-warranted batteries cost the same, regardless of how much they weigh or how many plates are in them, or what their amp-hour capacity is. It's your money, get a big one.

Upon winter lay-up I rotate the battery into the car. I believe it is better to keep a battery working and regular than it is to let it sit around in the cellar or garage for a whole season. Leaving one on a trickle charger for an extended period of time is even worse for it. The less you move your true marine battery, the better. And when you do move any battery, don't bang it around. Stirring up sediments inhibits the necessary chemical reactions and reduces battery life.

### ANATOMY OF A BATTERY

The following illustrations are largely self-explanatory. The case consists of not only the outside shell, but the internal cell walls as well. Each cell is a separate box. Alternate positive and negative plates, with a separator between successive plates, are assembled into "elements"; one element goes into each cell. Lower-priced batteries use resin-impregnated cardboard separators; heavy-duty deep-cycle marine batteries use rubber or polyethylene separators and fiberglass mats to reduce shedding from the positive plate. The cell elements are electrically connected in series, by either internal or external connectors. The two end elements are connected to the terminals, positive and negative. And then a lid or cover containing the filler holes and vent caps is sealed on to the top of the case. All batteries are made this way. Next we'll look at what makes marine batteries different from the rest and why you'll have to pay for that difference. As with most other accessories we buy for our boat that truly are marine in construction and composition, you get what you pay for.

True marine batteries are always big, fat, ugly, and black.

No dainty pastel tops or ribbons or bows on these brutes. They are just as tough and mean as they look. Reach over to jerk one up off the ground and you're apt to end up with a hernia or a wrenched back. Surrette's most popular 12-volt marine model, HR-8D, weighs in at 165 pounds wet. All its Spe-

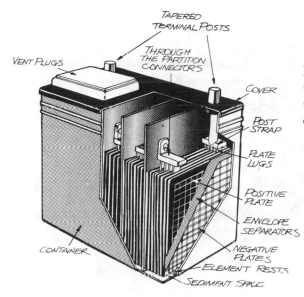

**Figure 3–4:** *Each cell in the battery case is a separate compartment.*

TAPERED TERMINAL POSTS

THROUGH THE PARTITION CONNECTORS

VENT PLUGS

COVER

POST STRAP

PLATE LUGS

POSITIVE PLATE

ENVELOPE SEPARATORS

NEGATIVE PLATES

ELEMENT RESTS

CONTAINER

SEDIMENT SPACE

**Figure 3–5:** *Alternating positive and negative plates, with a separator between each, are assembled into an element.*

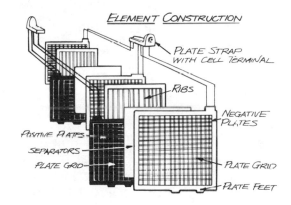

ELEMENT CONSTRUCTION

PLATE STRAP WITH CELL TERMINAL

RIBS

NEGATIVE PLATES

POSITIVE PLATES

SEPARATORS

PLATE GRID

PLATE GRID

PLATE FEET

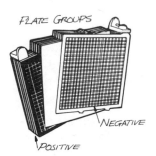

PLATE GROUPS

NEGATIVE

POSITIVE

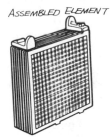

ASSEMBLED ELEMENT

**Figure 3–6:** *One element assembly is put into each cell.*

**Figure 3–7:** *A marine grade 12-volt battery. (Courtesy of Surrette Storage Battery Company, Inc.)*

cial Heavy Duty Series 400 batteries are heavyweights. The *lightest* of the marine group is a hefty 65-pounder. If we compare this with a Sears DieHard, a widely-distributed premium brand, I find in my latest catalog that the heaviest auto model is 46 pounds, the heaviest marine type weighs 51 pounds, and the heaviest commercial grade is a 54-pounder.

Weight is one thing, and I believe the most obvious of the specifications as far as the average boatowner is concerned. But a battery's electrical performance is more properly rated in terms of actual discharge capabilities. The industry-wide standards set for new fully charged batteries are as follows:

20-HOUR RATE—The number of amps that can be withdrawn at a constant rate for 20 hours at 80° F (26.7° C) before voltage drops below 1.75 V/Cell.

RESERVE CAPACITY—The number of minutes for which a constant 25 amperes may be withdrawn at 80° F (26.7° C) before voltage drops below 1.75 V/Cell.

COLD CRANKING—The discharge in amperes that can be maintained for 30 seconds at 0° F (− 17.8° C) before voltage drops below 1.2 V/Cell (cold cranking doesn't usually have a direct significance in most boat operation, because boats are used mostly in warm weather, but there are exceptions).

These are the numbers that really tell the story about how the battery actually performs under the most demanding of conditions; they tell us how much guts a battery has.

You might think marine batteries are all 12-volt units these days, just like the cars. But that's not true. Lots of 6-volt batteries still are being manufactured, as well as 8-volt models. Perhaps you have noted on some electronic equipment specifications, 32 volts DC. The photos show an extra heavy duty 8-volt battery with its flag-type marine terminals, and how four of them have been strapped together in series to give the 32-volt total. This is common practice on larger commercial vessels. Note the four cells and four filler caps on the battery.

Figure 3–8: *Note the four cells and four filler caps on this 8-volt marine battery. (Courtesy of Surrette Storage Battery Company, Inc.)*

**Figure 3–9:** *The 32-volt DC system is often used on larger commercial vessels. Four 8-volt batteries are connected in series. (Courtesy of Surrette Storage Battery Company, Inc.)*

Why 32 volts? Less heat loss in the wires. Remember that power equals V × I. If the same power is carried at higher voltage, the current will be less. And power lost to heat in the wires is I²R. If I is less, so will be the power lost to heat.

## SIX-VOLT BATTERIES

Six-volt batteries are not made just for older boats, which have never converted to the more modern 12-volt system. In fact, these 6-volt EIGH-262 batteries are now being used in all Swan yachts built by Nautor of Finland, according to the battery manufacturer. They have extra thick 0.170-inch positive plates. Two of these in series give 12 volts, and more storage capacity than one single 12-volt battery. Another reason for buying two 6-volt batteries instead of a 12 is space. Surrette's marketing director told me that while the 20″ × 11″ × 10″ 12-volt HR-8D is the company's most popular model (current list price $356.30), when people don't have enough space he recommends 2 6-volt batteries, which take up less area but are taller. It costs only four dollars more to get the two six-volt batteries at today's prices, and they have thicker positive plates to boot. He wrote this note on back of the EIG-225 photo, "6

volt 225 A.H. capacity with .170 (170 thousandths) thick positive plates. Longer life (*over* 6 years) if maintained properly
and not discharged below 50% daily. Best *average* about 9
years." And I have seen copies of testimonial letters that state
that twice that lifetime for a good marine battery in commercial
service is not unusual.

A little note of optimism here. most boat batteries are, and
certainly should be, low in the hull, where temperature is low
and rather steady. These are very good conditions for battery
life, so ordinary "better"—i.e. 48-month—batteries may live
longer, too.

The true nature of marine starting and deep-cycle batteries
can be described succinctly:

    a. The more thin plates you put in one cell, the more surface
       area is exposed, and therefore, the more cranking capacity.
    b. Putting thick heavy plates in same cell size reduces the
       cranking (not needed in deep cycling) but gives much
       more reserve capacity. This can be overcome, however,
       by increasing battery size. You can have the best of both
       worlds.

That's good advice, and that's why I always buy the biggest
battery that will fit—big in size, big in weight, big number of
plates, and big in performance ratings. You can't go wrong buying BIG, as long as it will fit.

**Figure 3–10:** *Two 6-volt
marine batteries in series may
be more advantageous than a
single 12-volt battery on a
cruising boat. (Courtesy of
Surrette Storage Battery
Company, Inc.)*

## BATTERY BANKS

Most boatowners use more electricity aboard than we do, I know that. But hell, we started out with *none* back in 1974. We had kerosene running lights, kerosene cabin lights, a kerosene stove, a wood-burning heater, a lead line and a 15-foot pole for depth sounding, and I told all my friends that I would get a radio as soon as I found one that ran on kerosene. Things have changed. But I'm not sure always for the better, though. I succumbed to the lure of a few electronic doo-dads, for navigation and safety, of course. We haven't added much in the way of creature comforts—no TV yet, and the car stereo I did install got ripped-off the first year. Maybe I should have stuck with kerosene. But every once in a while, I get to thinking about building another, retirement live-aboard vessel, and I don't think I'll skip on creature comforts and conveniences in that boat.

Most new boats these days come with an assortment of electrical and electronic devices that would have been considered completely superfluous and extravagant just a few years ago. They all use power, and lots of it. Few serious cruising vessels can get by with only one battery any more. As soon as you need more than one you're into battery banks.

Of course the simplest bank is two; one for starting and the other for everything else. As we have already pointed out, the two types have different characteristics. Since most of us with a floating home can get away from cold weather, or batten down and snuggle up inside until spring, we seldom have to be concerned with real cold-weather starting problems.

A warm or temperate climate starting battery can well be a good 12-volt automobile type. That's what they are designed for, anyway. They start the engine, period. Then the alternator or generator cuts in, takes over the load plus recharges the battery. That's one side of your bank. The other side makes up the "house" or "ship's" batteries. This can be one unit or two, depending upon the total load. But these batteries must be of the deep-cycle type. The load imposed by navigation lights that burn all night, and cabin lights, and the compass light, and anchor light, the bilge pump, any water pumps, the electric MSD, etc., etc., etc. can do more serious damage to your storage system than the hundreds of amps used in starting. When your starting battery is low, but not fully discharged, the engine won't crank—and the battery will not be damaged. But leave a small cabin light on for a couple of days, and that ship's battery will completely discharge—to the point that recovery will be slow, and perhaps never complete. After 20 or 30 of these events, your auto battery will pack it in, no matter how many months are left on the warranty. A good marine deep-cycle battery will withstand hundreds of these charging cycles, though. That's what deep-cycle is all about.

## SELECTING A BATTERY

Your actual choice of batteries will depend on several things —how much can you afford to pay, how much space you have, and how much weight can you tolerate. Perhaps the real question you have to decide is, can you afford anything less than the best? As to two sixes or one 12-volt battery, I believe I'd favor the two sixes. When one cell dies, you can replace the 6 for half the cost of the 12, and have the benefit of more capacity throughout its entire life. None of these batteries will fit into those tacky plastic battery boxes anyway, so don't let that be a deterent to choosing the best. You'll have to design and build your own robust retainer assembly for the entire bank. Be sure to think about all the weight involved and what could happen to it in case of a knockdown, a capsize, or a pitchpole. Don't just ignore it and say, "It can't happen to me." It might.

No less a sailor than Sir Francis Chichester, the great solo circumnavigator, got into dreadful trouble because his extra-heavy battery was held down by its own case, not a box. In very heavy weather the case broke, and acid got loose—he had a terrible time cleaning it up before it damaged his wooden boat. Of course, he lost his electrics.

You control the battery through the Battery Switch. We'll talk more about that in Chapter 5—The Controls.

## BATTERY MAINTENANCE AND TOOLS

We've already talked about the hydrometer and its use. It's the most important battery tool you can have. Some other tools,

**Figure 3–11:** *Terminal puller, two terminal post cleaners and a carry strap.*

also purchased at a home and auto store, are shown in this photo.

No matter how good your battery is or how much you paid for it, if the terminals are dirty or corroded, it won't work properly. They must be kept shiny clean to insure good electrical contact. The cable clamps must be removed to be cleaned. That's what the terminal puller is for. I suspect that more batteries are damaged by not having one of these tools than anything else. Figure 3-12 shows a terminal puller tool in action.

Here's how to use one properly. First, loosen the cable clamp nut on the terminal. Then, squeeze the ears of the puller together to open the jaws, slip the open jaws over the cable clamp with the end of the screw centered on the post. Wind down the screw and the cable clamp will lift off the tapered terminal post. Don't ever try to beat the cable clamp off with a hammer or wrench or pry it off with a screwdriver; either technique may damage the terminal or the case. Then you're in big trouble. Let me add a word of caution here about terminal pullers. When you buy one, try it out well ahead of time, preferably in the store before paying for it. That's because there are some on the market (el cheapo models) that just don't work, even though they look like the unit in the illustration.

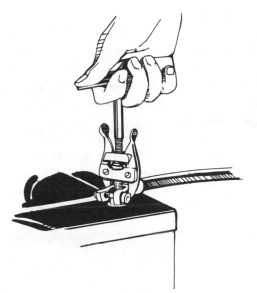

**Figure 3–12:** *The terminal puller is a must for avoiding damage to your battery. (Courtesy of Battery Council International.)*

Both cleaning tools shown in Figure 3-11 are used to clean the inside of the cable clamps as well as the surface of the terminal posts. One is a scraper-reamer (the four armed one) and the other is a wire brusher. Don't take off too much metal. Quit when the surfaces are shiny and reassemble. A little petroleum jelly or oil will help to prevent future corrosion.

The carry strap shown is OK for lightweight batteries, but not for heavy-duty ones. It is self-locking as long as used properly, as shown, with the little latch on top. That prevents it from slipping on the tapered post. But it will put too much pressure on the posts of a heavyweight battery. For those you'll have to rig your own rope sling if they don't come equipped with handles. Replacing a battery bank with new heavy-duty marine batteries is no mean task. Loading them aboard and stowing them below is hard work. You might want to rig a handy-billy tackle with a double and single block to give yourself an assist.

Be careful when handling batteries. Remember what we said about that back in the Preface. I don't mean to poke fun at someone's misfortune, but I'll never forget what I saw happen one day about 12 years ago. I repeat it now because there's a lesson here for all of us. It was spring outfitting time. The yard gang had just launched this English fellow's sailboat and put it on his mooring. He rowed out with his battery and some other gear, came alongside, stood up and reached over to pick up the battery. Everything was OK until he leaned over to push it up onto the sailboat. That's when the old physics laws about levers took over. The dinghy went out from under him, and he went into the water clutching the battery firmly—straight to the bottom. Soon he emerged, clambered aboard the sailboat—without the battery, of course—caught his breath, and then watched the wind blow his dinghy toward shore. Two guys who were gathering quahogs waited for it. He waved to them and hollered thanks for rescuing it for him. Then he watched them throw it on their pickup truck and drive away—never saw them or the dinghy again. Or the battery.

Here are eight tips for maximizing your battery's life:

1. Keep it charged.
2. Don't overcharge (more on this in Chapter 7).
3. Keep the electrolyte level full.
4. Use mineral-free water to fill battery cells.
5. Keep terminals clean.
6. Always use a terminal puller tool.
7. Don't move a battery any more than necessary.
8. Keep it cool and dry, preferably in a well-secured battery box.

## CHAPTER 4

# THE WIRING

## Electrical Veins and Arteries

If the battery is the heart of our boat's electrical system, then the wiring is the circulatory system—the arteries and veins for electrons. In our houses, the electrical wires, once installed and inspected, usually are forgotten for years or decades, and hardly ever cause a problem. Not so on our boats. Houses are not subjected to constant vibration, rolling, pitching, yawing, dampness, a hostile salt-air environment, and extremes of temperature. Boats are. And the wiring takes a beating. Some units, such as bilge pumps, are meant to run submerged. Running lights have to be exposed. Components mounted on the foredeck, such as an electric anchor windlass, are constantly subjected to salt water splashing and spray. And every wire that runs inside a hollow mast will be chafed and abraded from vessel motion. External connectors for mast wires and antennas are subject to moisture leaks and corrosion.

It's no wonder that wires can develop voltage drops and electrical leaks, in some cases dead shorts, considering the abuse they are given just because they happen to live on our boats.

### PROPER SIZE

The wiring carries charges from the battery, or other source, through the control devices, to the transducer, and then back to

**51**

the source. Ideally, the wires should have no resistance, but since this is impossible, we'll have to settle for minimum resistance. Back in Chapter 1, when we defined resistance, we found that it depended on three factors:

1. The resistivity of the metal
2. The length of the wire
3. The cross-sectional area of the wire.

Now it is time to talk about each of these factors in a little more detail.

## RESISTIVITY

Silver is the best conducting metal of all. But considering the price of silver these days, don't expect to find any wire made of it in your local hardware store. I remember back in World War II when an aluminum plant was built in our town, all the talk was about how the bus bars were pure silver. In very special high current applications, it may be worth the price to obtain the absolute minimum of resistance. But copper is 98% as good as silver is, and lot cheaper. That's why it is still the most used metal for electric conductors. Aluminum rates 61% of silver's conductivity value. It is often used in spite of this low value where weight is a critical factor, but not on boats. Since copper is the only type of wire we are apt to find available, we'll assume that resistivity is a constant, and not something that we'll have to concern ourselves about in selecting the proper size of wire.

## WIRE LENGTH

Length is important, and remember that the length includes both the "going there" and the "coming back" lengths, because all the boat wiring is of the two-wire type. Never use metal of the boat hull or any part of it such as a sailboat mast for the return portion of a circuit, as is done in our automobiles all the time. On a boat it becomes an open invitation for a corrosion disaster to occur. If you're installing a new electric device, first decide where you want it to be located and make sure that you can get the wires to that location. Once you cut or drill holes in a molded headliner, it's a little late to find that you can't feed wires to that spot. If you can't find some internal passage that doesn't show, you can run them outside and then cover the exposed wires with a wire channel made of extruded plastic or a wood box section that you can make yourself with a router or dado blade.

Sailing Specialties, Inc. of Lexington Park, MD make some neat plastic wiring covers with all different kinds of corner and "T" joints in both white and sandalwood colors. There also are some elegant teak channels in some chandleries and catalogs.

Now you have to figure where the device will be tied in to the electric supply. If you have some extra unused circuits on your control panel, you're home free. That's where the other ends of the wires will lead to. Next, measure the actual distance along the route of the wires between the control panel and the chosen location. Use your flexible ruler or a flat metal "snake" to make sure the route is open all the way, and not blocked by some unseen bulkhead or other obstruction. Do this first, and don't assume anything—that's the best way I know of to avoid problems later.

Now add up all the straight runs and jogs around obstacles to get the actual wire length from the panel to the device, and then double it and add a couple more feet to find how much wire you'll have to round up to make the installation. Why all

**Figure 4–1:** *Wiring covers.*

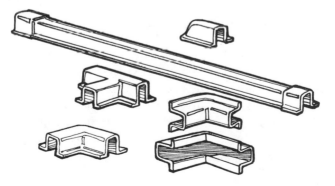

the careful measuring, and then adding a couple more feet? Well, it's always better to find that you have a foot too much wire than it is to find a foot too little. This is not a trivial point. If you're just a little short, there is a tendency to want to pull on the wire to stretch it just a little bit to get the kinks out, but that's just asking for trouble. Wire under tension is more apt to fail in use from abrasion or vibration, and the constant strain on the connector may cause the device to fail in time. The wires will have to be supported every 18 inches with plastic hangers or rubber-lined metal clamps to keep them from chafing, but the wires should be free from strain and "comfortable."

It is possible to find "two-conductor" wire, but not the common lamp cord variety, in some hardware stores. Lamp cord wire usually indicates the work of a lubber on a boat. The kind I mean, and sometimes use on board, has two separately insulated wires of proper AWG size twisted together and then fiber wrapped and finally coated with a plastic insulating sheath. I find this wire holds up well and gives me good service for a reasonable price.

## THICKNESS

The third factor is cross sectional area. In general, the thicker a wire is (the metal, not the insulation), the lower is its resistance. Since wires are usually some small fraction of an inch in diameter, the common measure used is the "mil" or thousandth of an inch. I guess electricians didn't like geometry, because they found a way to get rid of having to use pi, the ratio of a circle's circumference to its diameter, in calculating cross sectional area. They just invented another kind of area unit called the "circular mil," where the diameter squared gives the circular mil area. A wire with a diameter of 1 mil has an area of 1 circular mil. If the diameter is 2 mils, the area is 4 circular mils, etc. But the most common way to express wire "size" is by the American Wire Gauge (AWG) convention, originally set up for solid copper conductors only, but now used for all wires. For boat use, wires should be stranded for flexibility to prevent vibrational fatigue (or cold working) failure. This table shows some often used wire sizes and their characteristics.

*Table 4-1*
**WIRE SIZES**

| AWG No. | DIAMETER (mils) | CIRCULAR MILS | OHMS PER 1000 FEET @ 77° F. |
|---|---|---|---|
| 0000 | 460 | 212,000 | .0500 |
| 000 | 410 | 168,000 | .0630 |
| 00 | 365 | 133,000 | .0795 |
| 0 | 325 | 106,000 | .1000 |
| 1 | 289 | 83,700 | .126 |
| 2 | 258 | 66,400 | .159 |
| 4 | 204 | 41,700 | .253. |
| 6 | 162 | 26,300 | .403 |
| 8 | 128 | 16,500 | .641 |
| 10 | 102 | 10,400 | 1.02 |
| 12 | 81 | 6,530 | 1.62 |
| 14 | 64 | 4,110 | 2.58 |
| 16 | 51 | 2,580 | 4.09 |

This table shows how thick wires, like four-aught (0000), have practically no resistance, and the smaller ones, such as No. 16, have 4 ohms per 1000 feet or 0.4 ohms in 100 feet. For a 5 amp current through 100 feet of No. 16 wire, the resulting voltage drop will be $V = I \times R = 5$ amp $\times 0.4$ ohm $= 2$ volts. If we have only 12 volts from the battery, 2 of them never get to the device—they are wasted in heating the wire. That's nearly a 17% loss! If you hook up your VHF radio with that wire, it may receive OK, but changes are that your transmissions will be poor, at best. That's what is behind the following two tables, which give proper wire sizes for various lengths of wire, depending on the amount of voltage drop you can tolerate for a particular installation. For some devices, such as cabin lights or pumps or fans, up to 10% voltage drop will have little effect on their functioning, so we can use a smaller wire size. Lorans, radios, depth sounders, and other sensitive electronic units should operate as close to full voltage as possible, so a 3% maximum voltage drop is permitted. Buy bigger wires to hook them up with.

*Table 4-2*
### AWG WIRE SIZE TO USE FOR A MAXIMUM 10% VOLTAGE DROP

| CURRENT (amps) | TOTAL WIRE LENGTH FOR ROUND TRIP DISTANCE IN FEET | | | | | | |
|---|---|---|---|---|---|---|---|
| | 10 | 20 | 30 | 40 | 50 | 60 | 70 |
| 5 | 18 | 18 | 18 | 16 | 16 | 14 | 14 |
| 10 | 18 | 16 | 14 | 14 | 12 | 12 | 10 |
| 15 | 18 | 14 | 12 | 12 | 10 | 10 | 8 |
| 20 | 16 | 14 | 12 | 10 | 10 | 8 | 8 |
| 25 | 16 | 12 | 10 | 10 | 8 | 8 | 6 |

Now, just how do we go about using these tables? Once we decide what line loss we can tolerate, whether 10% or 3%, and we know the round trip wire length we need, the only other thing we have to determine is the maximum current we expect to flow in the wire. To do that we need to know the wattage ratings of all the devices that will be connected in the circuit. Let's say it's a searchlight rated at 100 watts (look on the nameplate to make sure). Remember $P = I \times V$, so $I = P/V = 100$ watts/12 volts = 8.3 amps. Use the 10-amp row and go across to the closest length to find the proper wire size. For 10% drop and 30 feet of wire, this will be AWG 14. It would be AWG 10 for 3% drop. If several devices are to be connected in parallel, such as a set of cabin lamps, use the sum of all the wattages, just in case they are all on at the same time. Remember that if you use too small a wire, you will not be able to deliver full voltage to the device; energy will be lost as heat along the wire. Then there is a secondary effect that as the temperature of the

*Table 4-3*
### AWG WIRE SIZE TO USE FOR A MAXIMUM 3% VOLTAGE DROP

| CURRENT (amps) | TOTAL WIRE LENGTH FOR ROUND TRIP DISTANCE IN FEET | | | | | | |
|---|---|---|---|---|---|---|---|
| | 10 | 20 | 30 | 40 | 50 | 60 | 70 |
| 5 | 18 | 14 | 12 | 10 | 10 | 10 | 8 |
| 10 | 14 | 10 | 10 | 8 | 6 | 6 | 6 |
| 15 | 12 | 10 | 8 | 6 | 6 | 6 | 4 |
| 20 | 10 | 8 | 6 | 6 | 4 | 4 | 2 |
| 25 | 10 | 6 | 6 | 4 | 4 | 2 | 2 |

wire increases, so will its resistance. That's why a temperature of 77° F was specified in the first table. Resistance feeds on itself.

Even though the 10% table includes some number 18 wire sizes for low current short runs, I always make it a point to *never* use any wire smaller than AWG 16. (This is in keeping with many "official" recommendations: #16 is always given as the smallest permissible. Partly at least this is due to the mechanical weakness of the smaller sizes.) I never buy anything smaller, so I never have any aboard in my spare wire box where I might be tempted to use it in an inappropriate place. It is never improper to use a larger size than called for, just a little more expensive. However, there is an exception. Some devices, such as small sockets or receptacles, are built to accommodate small wires only. Attempts to use too large a wire have been known to cause "open circuits," i.e. one or both wires completely loose, or "short circuits" in which the two wires touch each other, allowing very excessive currents to flow, and blowing fuses. When using two-conductor wiring, remember that the round-trip length must be used in the tables to find the proper AWG size, but you need buy only half as much wire length, plus a foot or so.

## INSULATION

All hook-up wire used must, of course, be insulated. Both wires carry charge and energy to and from the device, and since they may run in close proximity to other wires, it is necessary to have all the wiring completely covered and insulated from any possible contact. Practically all insulation used on wire today is plastic, but there are several kinds of plastic in use. Some is "thermoplastic," other is "cross-linked polymer" (simply another plastic), and some other kind is oil-resistant, but can't be used in engine rooms because it has a lower operating temperature. The actual codes for insulation are specified by American Boat and Yacht Council, but in a practical sense knowing the proper code letter doesn't help Joe Boatowner very much when he goes to hook up his new depth sounder. What it does accomplish is to ensure that manufacturers complying with those standards will deliver the proper goods to our favorite marine store. Once again, it's a case of sticking with quality and relying on the good name and reputation of the manufacturer. Most insulation is routinely tested to withstand "breaking down" at 600 volts, i.e. allowing current to pass through it, even though it will be used in a 12-volt system; so don't be upset if the clerk sells you some wire with "600 V" stamped on it, along with the wire size. Radio Shack sells hookup wire packs, but its largest wire size is 18 gauge, less than I recommend for boat use. It does carry heavy-duty 12-gauge wire (in red and black) in 20-foot lengths.

## IDENTIFICATION CODES

The first time you look inside your control panel or see the wad of wires emanating from it, you'll probably be flabbergasted and wonder how in the world anyone can tell which one goes where. Of course, the electricians who work in the boat factory know, that's their job. And when they are doing the wiring, everything is exposed, so it's easy to trace along the entire circuit. In most cases, everything mounted on deck is attached and wired before the deck is assembled to the hull, and interior overhead fixtures, such as lights, are wired in place before the headliner is attached to the underside of the deck. Some builders use a wiring "harness" or preassembled and shaped wire bundle in which all the wires for the designated standard electrical devices are included. But many others do not. Some run the wires in a special wire bin or trough along both sides of the boat, with access ports to get at the wires in case you ever need to. But many others do not. If you happen to own one of those "other" type boats, you cannot count on being able to get at all the wires. For example, if the cabin light wires run on top of the headliner, then when the liner is glassed to the deck and the deck assembled to the hull, you'll probably never see that wire again. If it ever gives you trouble, you will likely not be able to remove it or to fish a new one into its place. You'll most likely just have to cut off the ends and run a new replacement wire in by another route. Many, many boats have been built this way, so don't think you are the only one to get a bum wiring package.

There is a "Recommended Marine Wiring Color Code for DC Under 50 Volts" established by the American Boat and Yacht Council. It includes some 14 different colors that are to be used for specific types of wiring installations. But these are only recommendations, and the public has no way of knowing whether the builder complied with all, none, or some of the code. A few of the uses and colors specified are:

| Red | Positive Mains | Dark Blue | Cabin Lights |
|-----|----------------|-----------|--------------|
| White | Return, | Brown | Pumps |
| or Black | Negative Mains | Dark Gray | Nav. Lights |
| Green | Bonding | Pink | Fuel Gauge |
| Yellow | Bilge Blower | Purple | Ignition |

You can check the back of your control panel to see whether you can find these colors used on the labeled circuits. If so, you're in luck if you ever have to trace out a circuit to troubleshoot it. But I don't know any boatbuilder who will shut down the assembly line because they ran out of pink or purple wire. Besides, it will be impossible to find the proper color wire in any retail outlet if you want to do some of your own wiring. Sometimes it's hard enough just getting the right size wire, let alone color. With luck, you can occasionally find a variety of colors in an automotive supply store; they often stock gauges 10 to 14 in a variety of colors, but you may have to buy a whole spool of each color. We'll talk more about how to do this in the Troubleshooting Section. But, once you determine which wire goes where, you should label it with a sticky plastic letter or number tape marker from an electric supply store, or a piece of masking tape with your own ID marker.

## TERMINALS

Terminals are used to hook up the wires. They are the fittings attached to the ends of the wires and come in a variety of sizes, shapes and types. Some are bare metal, usually meant to be soldered to the wire. Some are insulated, and are meant to be crimped to the wire end with a special tool. I prefer to solder these as well as crimping them; maybe that's like wearing a belt and suspenders, too, but I do it anyway. Often the insulated fittings are color coded according to the wire size as follows:

|        |               |        |
|--------|---------------|--------|
| RED    | AWG 22 TO 16  | SMALL  |
| BLUE   | AWG 16 TO 14  | MEDIUM |
| YELLOW | AWG 12 TO 10  | LARGE  |

The photo shows a handy assortment of solderless terminals as well as the tool for crimping them. Actually, the tool will cut the wire, strip the insulation, and then crimp the terminal. A different notch is used for each different color to obtain the proper crimp. I just don't trust crimping alone in the salt air environment. Soldering seals the connection as well as strengthens it.

I always carry a rechargeable soldering iron aboard *Integrity* when we are off cruising. It holds a charge for about 6 weeks, and is easily recharged overnight whenever some household

**Figure 4–2:** *In spite of the name, solder the solderless terminal assortment after crimping to avoid future problems. Never use acid-core solder or acid flux.*

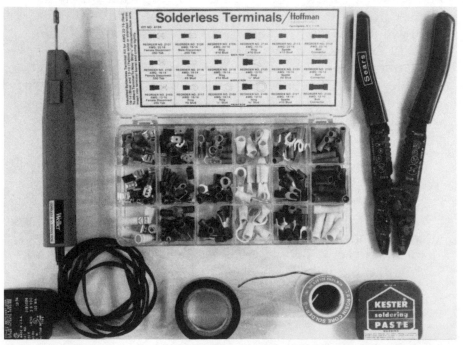

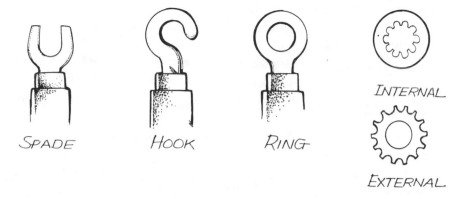

**Figure 4–3:** *Spade, ring and hook terminals and two star washers.*

AC is available. The small tip heats up very quickly and does a good job. The solder and flux are standard items available at any electric, electronic, or hardware store. Make sure that the solder is *rosin core. Never* use acid flux or acid core solder for any boat electrical work; that will just invite corrosive destruction. If you overheat the insulation it will decompose, forming the same acidic products, and leading to the same troubles later on. If the insulation turns black and gooey, let the joint cool and wipe off a few times with rubbing alcohol or even vodka (yes!). This will at least reduce the acidity.

Some terminals are "spade" or open ended. You merely loosen the hold down screw, slip the spade under the screw head, and retighten. But if the screw should loosen, the spade terminal could slip out just as easily and fall off. That's why I don't normally use them. Ring terminals can't fall off, but the screw must be completely removed and then reinstalled through the ring. It's easy to drop those little devils, and when you do, they always seem to land in the bilge. If you can, drape a rag or towel under where you are working to catch any small parts that might fall. Make sure you use a lock washer on top of the ring and under the screw head. A brass or bronze star washer works best here, rather than a split-type lock washer. If the screw should ever loosen on a light circuit, the light will flicker when the terminal wiggles, making and breaking the circuit. You will know something is loose, but the ring will not fall off until the screw backs completely out. You should have found the trouble before then. A hook terminal is in between the spade and ring—better than the spade, but not as good as the ring. If it's all I have on hand, I'll use one until I get some more rings and then replace it.

## INSTALLATION

Now let's recap this chapter by going back to that searchlight we were talking about earlier and hooking it up so it will work. It was 100 watts, drawing 8.3 amps, and the wire specified was 30 feet of No. 14, meaning the location is about 15 feet from the control panel. A spare circuit was still available, with a fuse, we'll assume. We'll not be concerned with the mechanical fastening of the unit to the cabin top or flying bridge here. The way the wiring is done will depend upon the way the light is constructed. If it is a single unit design it can be hard-wired from the panel to the light with the wire coming up through the mounting block on the bottom. That way the wire will not show. If the light is demountable so it can lift off the base, I would wire it through a watertight bulkhead connector. That way the light can be removed and stowed below where it might not be stolen. A short "pigtail" lead will run from the light to the connector.

Strip a quarter-inch of insulation from each wire end, insert the wire into the barrel of a blue-colored terminal of proper size (choices are #6, #8, #10, or ¼-inch studs), and crimp tightly with the tool by squeezing. Wait a minute! Let's see if you caught that reference to *Stud Size*. This is NOT the same as the wire size, which was indicated by the color of the terminal's insulating sleeve. Stud size refers to the size of the opening or hole in the attaching end of the terminal, which is determined by the size of the stud it must slip over, or the machine screw that must pass through it to hold it in place. These are the clearance hole sizes for the various stud or screw diameters.

|  |  |
|---|---|
| #6 | .147 inch |
| #8 | .173 inch |
| #10 | .204 inch |
| ¼ inch | .2656 or ¹⁷⁄₆₄ inch |

Just remember that you have two choices to make when it comes to picking out a terminal to put on a wire—the size of the wire it must crimp onto and the size of the stud or screw that attaches it.

After crimping I would heat the terminal and flow some solder into the joint as well. Route the wire as you planned and support it with plastic hangers every 18 inches. Install some anti-chafe tape wherever it passes through a hole or slip a piece of hose or tubing over it, which is even better. Now open the control panel to secure the other ends of the wires. One (red, according to the color code) will go to the positive feed at the switch you are using. The other (black or white) will attach to the negative bus bar. Attach the proper blue terminals, as before, use a star lock washer under each screw head and tighten securely. Make sure there is a 10-amp fuse in the fuse holder. Turn on the switch and the light should come on like the sun. Contratulations. That wasn't so hard, was it?

## A LESSON IN SOLDERING

We told you that this was going to be a nitty-gritty nuts and bolts kind of a book. So now it's time to get out some tools and practice how to do some of the things we've been talking about. Nothing is more fundamental to doing practical electrical work than learning how to solder correctly. The two key words to good soldering are CLEAN and SHINY. You can't get good results with dirty tools or wires, and a proper solder joint will be shiny bright. If it doesn't look right, it probably isn't. And if it isn't just right, it probably will cause you trouble in the future. The only way I know to learn to solder is to do it. The more you practice, the better you will get.

Put the book down for a while and go round up your supplies. Get some wire—any old kind will do for practice, but stranded is better, because it's the only kind you should use on your boat. Get a knife or crimper-stripper tool, some sandpaper, your soldering gun or iron, a small can of soldering paste, and some solder—rosin core only, NEVER acid core. A spool of solder is easier to work with than a loose wad because it can serve as its own holder, thus freeing up one of your hands. It is better to get your solder from an electronics store than a general hardware store. Then you know it is the proper electronic type, rosin core, low melting point with higher tin content (usually 60% tin and 40% lead). In a hardware store you are apt to get plumber's solder—more lead, higher melting point, and probably acid core or no flux core. The paste is for preparing the soldering iron or gun by "tinning."

The tip of your iron or gun must be clean and shiny bright in order to do good work with solder. Tinning means coating the tip with a thin even coat of solder. With a piece of fine sandpaper or emery cloth clean the tip of all crusty residue from former jobs. When it is good and clean dip it into the paste to get a very light coating, not too much. Plug in the iron and heat it up. The paste cleans the surface and prevents oxides from forming, which could prevent the solder from adhering. When hot, touch the end of the solder wire to the tip and allow it to flow on as a smooth coating. Shake off any excess while hot. The tool is now tinned and ready for use. Note the shiny silvery look of the tip. That's what you have to look for on all good solder work. If the joints are dull or lumpy, they're no good. Lumpy indicates a "cold joint"—the solder melted, but did not penetrate; that usually means the work was not sufficiently heated.

Next is the wire. It has to be prepared, too. You can't solder dirty wire. A freshly exposed wire that has just been stripped of its insulation is usually clean enough. If it's not clean, pull it through some sandpaper or scrape with the edge of your knife blade. You must never rely on the solder to make a joint for you. Solder's function is to bind and seal the joint. A mechanically sound joint must exist before any soldering is done. The joint is made by twisting the clean wires together. Then they can be soldered. If some two-conductor wires are being spliced together, you can avoid the problem of ending up with a big bulky joint by staggering the two splices a few inches as shown in Figure 4-4 and by using a modified Western Union splice to join each wire.

A true Western Union splice is made with only solid conductors, so I call this one a modified version. I like it better than the rat-tail joint because it lies flatter and is less bulky when

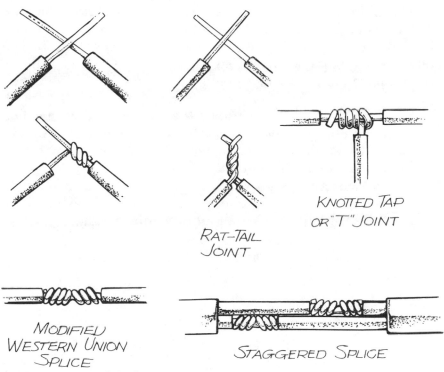

Figure 4–4: *Modified Western Union, rat tail, knotted tap or T and staggered splice wiring joints.*

finished and taped. The sketches show how to make both of them.

When tieing into an existing wire use a T or tap joint. This joint can be made stronger by "knotting" it as follows: the stripped end of the branch wire goes around the exposed main wire from behind, crosses behind the branch wire and then wraps around the main on the other side in short tight turns. When soldered and taped, this joint will survive considerable abuse for a long time.

Now that we have tinned the iron and made the joint, we're ready to solder it. This is done by putting the hot iron or gun to the joint to heat it up. Then touch the solder wire to the other side of the wire joint, not to the hot iron. If you have to hold the joint in one hand and the iron in the other, how do you hold the solder? Let the spool hold it for you. Unroll a couple of inches and bend over the end to a convenient working height. Then push the joint against the solder with pressure from the hot iron. Do it that way as you practice all these things. On board, you might not have enough room to do it that way all the time. I have held the solder in my mouth and then leaned over to push it against the hot joint. Where there's a will, you'll figure out a way. Just remember that the wire must be hot enough to melt the solder or else it won't flow into the strands properly. If you melt the solder with the gun, then it will just sit on the outside of the wire like a lump and usually cool with a dull surface. Always inspect the soldered joint as soon as it cools to make sure it is a good one. Remember the key words— bright and shiny. If it looks right, it probably is right.

## CHAPTER 5

# THE CONTROLS

## Brains Of The System

### THE CONTROL PANEL

Continuing our electrical system anatomy lesson, we next come to the brain, the control panel. The battery was the heart, pumping the electrons around the circuit; the wiring was the arteries and veins, carrying the charges around your boat; and now the control panel exercises jurisdiction over where those charges will be sent. It may also be designed to give us information about the state of the batteries' charge, as well as control over which battery will be selected for use at any given time.

If your boat was home-built, or was originally purchased without any electrical system, you can buy the components to assemble your own control panel from scratch, as I did for *Integrity*. Or, you can buy a blank panel from your favorite marine store for a fairly reasonable price. A panel with fuses runs considerably less money than one with circuit breakers, but you have to realize that they are not the same thing, even though they both serve the same function. Two good circuit breakers alone will cost nearly as much as a cheap complete fused switch panel. A simple 5 or 6-circuit plastic or aluminum board panel with switches and fuses is priced from $35 to $50 in 1984; you can find cheap imports for about half that in discount catalogs. A comparable simple circuit breaker unit is a little over $100.

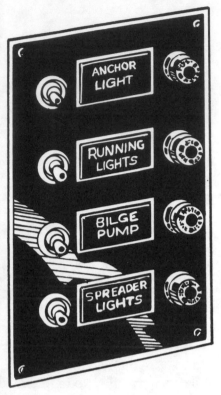

**Figure 5–1:** *A fuse-protected control panel.*

**Figure 5–2:** *Marinetics model DELTA accessory control panel is supplied with circuit breakers rated 5, 10, 15 and 20 amps, but can readily be changed to meet owner's needs up to 50 amp rating. (Courtesy of Marinetics Corporation.)*

As you can see from Figures 5-1 and 5-2, both types are meant to be mounted flush. You will have to cut a hole in the cabin liner or ceiling or a bulkhead—but make sure the bulkhead does not back up to an enclosed fuel or engine compartment. Before you cut the hole, make sure there is enough clearance behind it to fit the components in back of the panel. The circuit breaker units are deeper than the fuses, so they will require more clearance. Also, remember to make certain that you have a clear run for all the wires from the battery and to each of the circuits. If there is not enough clearance where you want to mount the panel, don't despair, just build a wooden frame to the outside panel dimensions and with sufficient depth. Secure it to the liner or bulkhead, cut a hole for the wires to pass through, and you're in business.

## WHERE TO PUT IT?

Where should the panel be located? No matter what type of panel you choose, these recommendations from Marinetics Corporation, originators of the modern pleasure-craft circuit breaker panel concept, are excellent.

1. Locate as centrally as possible relative to functional oper- ation of the yacht and to the yacht's battery banks.
2. Do *not* locate on a bulkhead backing up to an enclosed fuel or engine compartment.
3. Do *not* locate in an exposed area which receives direct water spray—this principle applies to all electrical equip- ment.
4. When possible, locate at or near eye level. Human engi- neering studies reveal that operation of any equipment is facilitated when operating controls are readily visible.

Even if you build your own panel, do a neat job, give it a nice finish, and put it on display where it will be regularly used. Perhaps you are thinking that many sailboat builders seem to ignore number 3 above when they locate the control panel just inside the companionway, where it is subject to getting wet by rain, drizzle and salt spray during a slog to weather. Their main concern is putting the boat together as simply and as inexpen- sively as possible, not the long-term survival of your control panel. That location is near the engine (if an inboard), and near the battery, which often is located under a quarter berth.

When electric lights, etc. are prewired inside the headliner, the wires will run to the companionway on top of it. They are the ones you probably won't be able to replace when the boat is all assembled. There is method to the madness of doing it that way, but it is not always to the boatowner's benefit.

The panels we have been looking at and describing should be adequate for most yachts, both sail and power, up to about 34 feet in length, or longer, if you are not so addicted to things electrical. If you are living aboard a vessel 34 feet or more in length, you are apt to run out of circuits rather quickly. When that happens, it is easier to add a second panel—which I would recommend, even though you end up with three or four "spare" circuits. If you have outgrown the first panel, it is a sign you are becoming more dependent upon electricity, and your needs will likely expand as you find other attractive devices to incorporate into your life afloat.

### REPLACEMENT ALTERNATIVES

The other alternative to installing a second panel is to buy a larger replacement model, with some other features than just switches and circuit protectors already built in. If you plan to spend a lot of time aboard this boat and keep it as a long term investment, this makes sense. But I certainly wouldn't go. through all the trouble for a boat you only expect to keep two years. It is possible to economize on the number of circuits in use by combining several devices into one circuit—but there's a danger to this. Remember how we chose the proper size wire back in the last chapter? Wire size depended on both total current and total length. You can't just install a bigger circuit breaker or fuse, and then add some more lights or electronics to one of the existing circuits. You'll have to first recalculate the new total current and then, most likely, rewire the entire circuit. This can be a mess, but it is less expensive than buying new panels. If you go this route, plan ahead, and use some logical grouping of components in the same circuit—compass light with the navigation lights, since they will be used at the same time; depth sounder with other navigation electronics; stereo with cabin lights, etc. It wouldn't make much sense to combine the searchlight with a bilge pump, would it? Control panels can be as simple or as complex as you desire. It all depends upon the thickness of your wallet. We'll come back to panels later, after we have looked at some other control devices.

## SWITCHES

We have been talking about switches as a part of the control panel, but we haven't really taken a close look at them. Let's do that now. None of them will look like the symbol for a switch, the old knife-blade variety. If you should ever happen to find one of those relics on a boat, replace it immediately. The switch itself is fail-proof, but it has a bad habit of arcing or making a spark when it breaks the circuit, and since the switch is open to the air, any gasoline fumes or propane leaks could be ignited. That should be enough to convince you to get rid of the switch. As long as we are talking about the possibility of arcing, I should mention that on board a gasoline engine boat, whenever switches are to be used in enclosed engine or fuel tank compartments, they must be specially constructed to conform to U.S. Coast Guard specifications, for "ignition protection" and be tested and listed by Underwriters Laboratories (U.L.). Look for the UL label to make sure. All switches designated for "marine use" will cost more than close look-alikes displayed at your local discount auto supply store. The president of Cole Hersee Company, a major U.S. manufacturer of electrical products for industrial, farm, automotive, and marine applications, said true marine electrical devices are designed for marine battery powered or low-voltage operation. Every operation of Cole Hersee switches, he said, performs a wiping or 'self-cleaning' action so that contact surfaces are prepared for maximum current-carrying capacity. True marine switches are made of brass and other non-ferrous components.

Once again we are reminded that you get what you pay for. The switches used in control panels are of the toggle or rocker

**Figure 5–3:** *Toggle switch for marine use. (Courtesy of Cole Hersee Company.)*

type, as shown. If you ever have to replace one of these, be sure to check for the proper current-carrying rating. It should be marked on the device or the package it comes in. If you can't find the information, don't use the switch.

## MASTER SWITCH

The biggest switch in your boat will be the master battery switch, the one place where you can go to shut off all battery power. Some models can be locked with a key in the OFF position. The master switch should be located in a readily accessible position as close to the batteries as possible. If you ever have to go buy the wire to hook one up, you'll see why. It is thick and expensive, so keep the runs short. In past years, battery switches, like Henry Ford's Model Ts, came in only one color, black. But now they may be red, gray or black. The red color does help locate the switch in a hurry, like when you have to shut off all electricity in case of a fire. They are larger than most other switches because of the size of the internal components—the connectors and conductors are built to carry the extremely large currents delivered to the engine starter. Here's another case where, if you have to replace one of these switches, you shouldn't just go looking for the cheapest one around. Check the specs. Make sure the replacement is as good, or better, than the original. Actual current values vary some with different manufacturers, but battery switches generally come in three ratings:

|  | CONTINUOUS DUTY | MOMENTARY |
|---|---|---|
| STANDARD | 250 AMPS | 350 AMPS |
| HEAVY DUTY | 350 AMPS | 600 AMPS |
| EXTRA HEAVY DUTY | | |
| (ON/OFF ONLY) | 600 AMPS | 1000 AMPS |

Your choice will depend mostly on the size and compression of your engine. It is a lot easier to crank a gasoline Atomic 4 than a Ford or GM diesel. The Guest Corporation, one well-known manufacturer of these switches, advises. "For proper size battery switch, your engine's cold cranking amperage should be lower than the momentary rating of switch." In picking a switch, there is another choice you should look for, "alternator field disconnect." A charging alternator or generator must never "look at" an open circuit, i.e. its load circuitry should always be "on." If you should inadvertently turn the switch to the OFF while the engine was running, you could seriously damage the alternator or generator. Battery selector switches without field disconnect all have the message "STOP ENGINE BEFORE SWITCHING OFF" clearly embossed on their face, to remind you not to do that. Switches with field disconnect interrupt the alternator field current, thus shutting off the alternator output, before the switch gets to the OFF position. All master battery switches should be "ignition protected" and UL approved.

If you have more than one battery aboard, you undoubtedly have a battery selector switch, which is another version of the master switch. Instead of just OFF and ON, these switches include OFF, 1, BOTH and 2 positions. This allows you to select either battery at any time, use both batteries in parallel if needed for starting the engine, or to completely disconnect both batteries. Some models have a key-lock OFF as well. Selector switches must be of the "Make Before Break" design; the other battery is always connected into the circuit before the

**Figure 5–4:** *Alternator field disconnect battery selector switch. (Courtesy of The Guest Corporation.)*

**Figure 5–5:** *Alternator field disconnect type of locking battery selector switch.*

first is removed, assuring that one battery is always on line, and hence that the alternator is always under load, as in the previous paragraph.

## FUSES

A fuse is a piece of wire having a low melting temperature. Fuses used on boats enclose the wire in a narrow glass tube with metal caps on the ends, like some auto fuses. When a circuit carries current in excess of its rated or fused value, the $I^2R$ heat produced (in the fuse, not in the whole circuit, we hope) will cause the fuse wire to melt, which breaks the circuit to protect it. So the fuse is nothing more than an automatic switch. Some people think that fuses are old fashioned, but I like them. They're always fail safe. They can't hang up or fail to function. Even when corrosion occurs on the end caps, the circuit stops working, and the circuit is protected. The only problem with fuses is that you have to carry spares for each different current rating. But they can be found in any auto supply store. Just be sure to ask for TYPE AGC or TYPE 3AG, which are all an inch and a quarter long; other kinds, such as

TYPE SFE, vary in length, and won't work in your fuse holders.

If a circuit includes a motor, such as a refrigerator, a blower or pump, or car-type vacuum cleaner, the fuse should be of the "slow-blow" type, so that the momentary inductive surge that occurs when motors are turned on will not blow it. You can find slow-blow fuses at any electronics store. To remove the fuse from its holder in the control panel, grip the cap between your fingers, push in slightly and rotate it about one-sixth turn to the left or counterclockwise. The fuse will come out with the cap. Check it by holding it up to the light to see if the wire looks intact. If a very heavy overload like a dead short blew it, the glass may be clouded or smoky—not much doubt about it being bad then. But a slow blow may melt the wire right next to the cap where it is hard to see. You can check it out for sure with a continuity test, which we'll talk about in Chapter 8. Whenever I remove a fuse from its holder, I always wipe it off with a rag or paper towel dampened with a shot of WD-40 or some other penetrating oil before returning it to service. Salty perspiration on your fingers might cause it to start corroding as it hides in the fuse holder. Not all fuses will be found in the control panel, though. Most electronic devices will have their own fuse, either built into the case and usually accessible from the rear, or located in the positive feed wire. It is possible to add single line fuses to each new circuit if you expand your system, but if you do this more than once or twice, in a year or two you won't remember where they are next time one of them blows and you're looking for it in the dark. It is best to keep all fuses in one place, the control panel. Then you can arrange to store the spare fuses of each required size nearby. You might even stick them next to the panel with some Velcro tape.

**Figure 5–6:** *Fused line connector.*

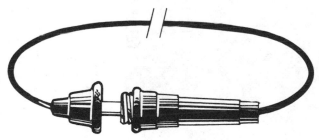

## CIRCUIT BREAKERS

If you want to avoid carrying spare fuses with you all the time, and if you want to simplify your control panel, you can use circuit breakers for protection rather than fuses. They combine the switch and circuit interruption function in one unit, and are tripped open by either magnetic or heat sensors. The breaker itself is quite a bit larger and heavier than the fuse holder assembly, and costs considerably more. Their use is extremely simple. To activate a circuit, merely flip the breaker switch to the ON position. Flip back to OFF to deactivate it. If a current overload develops, the breaker will automatically trip open and the switch flips to the OFF position. Before you can reset the switch you must find the cause of the overload and cure it. If you don't, the breaker's internal construction will prevent resetting. You cannot override the protective mechanism by holding the breaker switch closed—it simply won't work. This type breaker is also known as "trip-free." Circuit breakers are designed to carry slight overloads for a short time, such as the momentary surge from a motor starting up. They automatically do the job of the slow-blow fuses. Marinetics Corporation of Newport Beach, California, has been building these units since 1967. One of their units combines the master battery switch and a battery monitor along with 6 breaker-protected circuits. Airpax, a division of the Phillips Corporation, also makes an extensive line of circuit breakers.

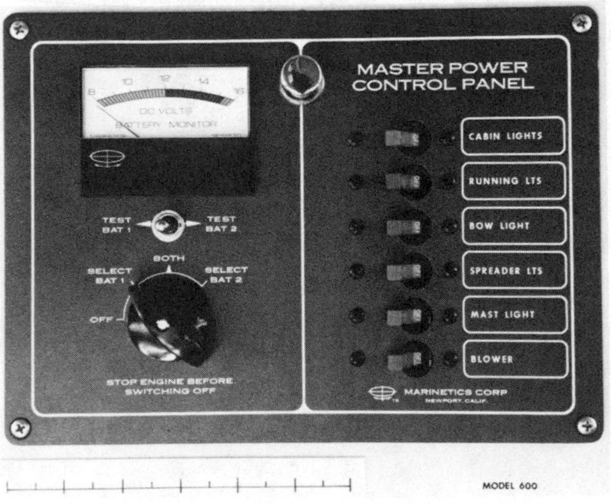

**Figure 5–7**: *Marinetics' model ALPHA is a complete DC control center. Note the reminder on the non-field disconnect type battery selector switch. (Courtesy of Marinetics Corporation.)*

## RELAYS

Relays, sometimes called solenoids, are electromagnetic switches that are used in high-current applications, especially engine starter circuits. Either a push-button momentary switch or an auto-type ignition key switch that engages the starter only when turned all the way—against spring pressure—is used to allow the operator to start the engine. The starter solenoid carries the heavy current from the starting battery to the starter, without having to route it all the way through the ignition switch itself or to the starter switch and back.

When the starter switch is closed a control current, small (15 amps) compared with the hundreds of amps in the starter current, flows through the solenoid coil, where it creates a strong magnetic field. The magnetic field pulls an iron plunger into the coil against spring pressure and its base bridges a gap between the two heavy-gauge copper contacts that carry the huge starting current to the starter. When the starter button is released, the control current dies, the magnetic field collapses, and the solenoid spring pushes the plunger out of the coil, breaking the starter circuit from the battery. Other relays can

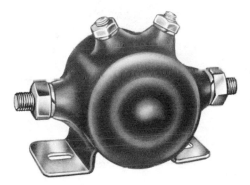

Figure 5–8: *Heavy duty marine solenoid encapsulated in sealed housing. (Courtesy of Cole Hersee Company.)*

Figure 5–9: *A solenoid schematic showing coil and contacts. (Courtesy of Cole Hersee Company.)*

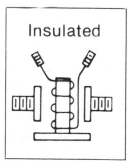

Insulated

be used whenever it is desirable to control a high-current circuit with a low current. You may find them used on compressor-driven air horns, electric anchor windlasses, etc.

## PANEL METERS

The master power control panel illustration shown a few pages back included a "DC Volts" battery monitor meter with a three-position, center-off switch used to test the condition of either battery. Note that it is an "expanded-scale suppressed-zero" meter. For a 0 to 15 volt meter, we don't need the first 11 volts to tell us anything about our batteries because by the time the voltage drops to 11 they are completely dead and depleted of useful charge. So we "suppress" the zero—actually the whole range of voltages 0–11. On the other hand, we are very interested in fractions of volts from 11 to (say) 16, so the scale is expanded between these values to give us better fractional readings. The following table shows the relationship between voltage and percent of charge, according to Battery Council International data.

| PERCENT CHARGE | OPEN CIRCUIT VOLTS |
|:---:|:---:|
| 100 | 12.6 or more |
| 75–100 | 12.4–12.6 |
| 50–75 | 12.2–12.4 |
| 25–50 | 12.0–12.2 |
| 0–25 | 11.7–12.0 |
| 0 | LESS THAN 11.7 |

Sometimes the meter is called a battery charge meter and then the scale shows only percent of charge, which is probably more meaningful to the average boatowner than volts. Most of us would probably think that on a 12-volt system, 6 volts is half full and zero is empty. But it's not that way at all.

A system ammeter may be included on the control panel also. Starting currents are never shown on a meter that is wired into a circuit. The ammeter may be center-zero, like our cars, to show both charging and discharging rates; or it may be left-end zero and show just the discharge current rate. If you should ever add a voltmeter to read the battery voltage at any time, remember that it will be connected across (in parallel with) the battery, and must draw some current all the time it is working. To avoid building in a constant drain on your system, you should hook it up in series with a "push to test switch" so it will give readings only when you want them.

---
# TRANSDUCERS
---

## Things That Do The Work

"**trans-duc-er** *n. Physics* Any device whereby energy may
be transmitted from one system to another system,
whether of the same or a different type."
    FUNK AND WAGNALL'S *STANDARD COLLEGE DICTIONARY*
    Harcourt, Brace & World, N.Y.


### WHAT DO YOU NEED?

Maybe "things that come on when you turn the switch" says
it more simply, and perhaps better, for most people. But still I
prefer to call them transducers. While many restrict the usage
of this word to things electronic, and particularly the interactive
part of the depth sounding system, the word really applies to
all energy converters.

As I mentioned earlier, if electricity didn't perform useful
functions for us, we wouldn't bother to have it on board. But
once we decide to become shipmates with it, then we must
guard against its taking over the vessel completely. More devices mean more circuits and a more complicated control panel
as well as more current. Soon we need more storage capacity,
more and/or bigger batteries, then it's a bigger alternator and/
or auxiliary generator—either gasoline, diesel, wind, water or
solar-powered. If you don't diligently guard against this kind of
overgrowth, you'll find yourself so loaded down electrically,
that generating it will require as much of your fuel as transport-
ing you from one cruising ground to the next. Your comfort

level may tie you to the end of a yellow umbilical cord forever. That's a terrible fate for any footloose cruiser.

How can you avoid electrical temptations? Think before you buy. When you see a new electrical device at a boat show or in a catalog that you believe could benefit your life afloat, pause and ask yourself these questions:

1. What is its power rating, or how much current will it draw?
2. How often will it be in use per day or per week? What will this add to your total Amp-Hour load? Can your present storage capacity handle it?
3. How will you wire it into your existing system? Is there a spare circuit, or can you parallel it with an existing one? Will that require rewiring? A new panel? Can you do that yourself, or will you have to hire a marine electrician to install it?
4. Do you really have room for it, or will it be in the way most of the time? Will the installation require extensive modification, carpenter work, special weldments, brackets, or other attachments?

If, after going through this whole list you decide you still want the item, then ask your mate what he or she thinks about it and your answers. You'd be surprised how many things you think are essential that your mate doesn't give a damn about and might even consider a waste of money or an unnecessary hindrance. If you mount your new satnav in the middle of her galley where she hits her head on it every time she uses the sink, you may find a wet dishrag hanging on it before long.

I would not be so foolish as to try to tell anyone what they need on their vessel. Everyone is different. And one's needs and desires change with time. A coastal cruiser that ties up at a marina most every night certainly has different needs from one that anchors out most of the time, or from an offshore cruiser that routinely makes long ocean passages, or a flat-out racing sailboat that tacks around the buoys a couple of times a week, or an outboard-powered bass boat used primarily for sport fishing, or a retired Maine lobster boat converted to family cruising. It makes a tremendous difference whether you use your boat on weekends and a two-week vacation each summer, or whether you take an early retirement and move aboard for a year or more. Only you can determine what you need.

## LIGHTS

Electric lights on a boat can be divided into three categories:

1. Navigation lights
2. Interior lights
3. Exterior lights

Of these, none are required to be electric, although it is now difficult to satisfy the new annex to the Rules of the Road concerning light specifications for larger vessels if your navigation lights are not electric.

### NAVIGATION LIGHTS

Most cruising boats come equipped with a set of navigation lights. On daysailers or runabouts they often come as an option. In some cases these factory choices may be of such inferior quality, or so poorly located that you might want to replace them. For sailboats up to 20 meters in length, the mast top tri-color (port, starboard, and stern) light for use while under sail alone is an excellent improvement in navigation lights. Don't get the tri-color confused with the masthead light, which still is required while under power.

I ordered my tri-color from England and had it installed and ready to go when they first became legal here a few years ago; you couldn't buy one in the U.S. at that time—nobody had them. One quartz-halogen bulb gives you all three lights, which are high enough and bright enough to be seen for miles, and cannot be obstructed by sails, lines or other deck items. I highly recommend this light, but don't throw away your other set. On a power boat, the masthead light can be wired with the other three navigation lights since they will always be used together. But on a sailboat, it must have its own switch, and used only when under power.

**Figure 6–1:** *Mast top navigation lights with tricolor on left and multifunction tricolor/anchor/strobe on right. (Courtesy of The Guest Corporation.)*

## INTERIOR LIGHTS

Interior or cabin lights come in many types, models and sizes. Kerosene cabin lamps give a soft glow besides some warmth, but you'll strain your eyes trying to read by them. An Aladdin kerosene lamp with a mantle is equal to a 60-watt electric bulb, but generates so much heat that you can only stand one below decks in the winter time. So most people use some kind of electric lights in their cabins. We tried one of those 6-volt lantern battery table lamps one summer. It seemed to give enough light to read by in the store, and did on the boat, too. But the battery lasted less than a week, and a replacement cost several dollars. It was the most expensive electricity I ever bought. We finally threw it away to save money. Don't repeat that folly. That brings us to cabin lights wired into the system.

The choices in style include dome, bulkhead, swivel, chart and bunk lights. The types include regular incandescent, high-intensity, "night vision" red, "glow" light, and fluorescent. In addition to choosing a style that blends with your cabin interior, check on the wattage of the bulb used in the light.

If you need a reading light, make sure you can install it where you like to read. Fluorescent lights give more light per watt than incandescent bulbs do, but they may interfere with loran reception. That's no big deal at anchor or in a slip, but might be underway at night, especially offshore when you might be relying on your electronic navigation equipment.

**Figure 6–2:** *Cabin dome light with built-in switch. (Courtesy of The Guest Corporation.)*

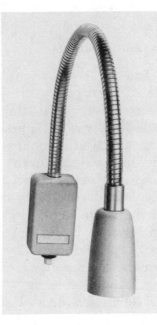

**Figure 6–3:** *Cabin and chart light with flexible neck for easy adjustment and a removable red filter. Use it to preserve night vision, remove for reading. (Courtesy of Guest Corporation.)*

**Figure 6–4:** *Bulkhead light fixture uses medium screw socket bulb. A marine shield or partial lamp shade clips over the bulb. (Courtesy of Perko, Inc.)*

A new fluorescent light has hit the market that produces no radio interference. It's a German import (Aqua Signal #33130) that I consider to be a breakthrough in 12-volt electrics. Power consumption is only 8 watts, but it produces as much light, according to the manufacturer, as a 20-watt bulb. Two of us can read by it with no difficulty. Turned on next to our loran, it produced no interference whatsoever.

## EXTERIOR LIGHTS

Exterior lights must be well sealed to be weatherproof. These include your compass light, spreader lights, small deck walkway lights, cockpit lights, anchor light, emergency survival lights, and a searchlight or spotlight.

Some of these lights, such as the anchor light, can be self-contained and dry-cell powered. Anchor lights can even burn kerosene. The survival lights have to be self-contained, to take with you in case you have to abandon ship or in case someone falls overboard. Searchlights or spotlights can be either hand-held or deck-mounted. Modern versions have either sealed-beam lamps or quartz-halogen bulbs; but all draw considerable current. A 100,000-candlepower (cp) quartz-halogen light will draw 4.3 amps, modest compared with a 300,000 cp sealed-beam unit at 12.5 amps or a 200,000 cp unit at 7.7 amps. Those

**Figure 6–5:** *Hand-held spotlight with swivel bracket. 200,000-candlepower spot, 50,000-candlepower flood. (Courtesy of The Guest Corporation.)*

current ratings should remind us to use these lights only inter-
mittently, but they surely are great for spotting channel buoys
or mooring pick-ups. Their light is so intense that we must be
constantly on guard to avoid shining them directly on other
moving vessels. If you blind an oncoming skipper, he may not
be able to avoid hitting you.

## MOTORS

We use more than a few electric motors on our boats. A motor
is a device that converts electrical energy into motion. What is
the difference between a motor and an engine? Engines convert fuel to motion. Motors transform one form of energy to
another. On a boat or ship, engine usually refers to the main or
primary propulsion mechanism. Motors are secondary motion
producers. Your gasoline or diesel *engine* is put into operation
by the action of the starting *motor.*

What makes an electric motor work? Magnetic forces. It is
another electromagnetic device. Electric currents passing
through various coils in the motor establish magnetic fields.
These fields interact with one another to produce motion. Without getting into all the intricacies of how different types of
motors are constructed and wired, let me just give you a few
basic principles for DC motors, which may be helpful in understanding, maintaining and troubleshooting the motor-driven
appliances on your boat. The few essential parts of a DC motor
are the armature, field, commutator and brushes. The armature,
or rotating portion of the motor, is usually a large cylinder of
soft iron or steel consisting of many thin layers, slotted, so as to
hold a number of copper wire coils, which make up the armature windings. Each coil is connected to a pair of insulated
segments of the cummutator, a rotary switch that turns with the
armature. Current is passed to and from the armature windings
by means of carbon brushes that make contact with the commutator. The external field in which the armature rotates is
established by another multipole electromagnet (the field), or
by permanent magnets. Those are the essential parts. This is
how they work:

1. Current flowing through the armature coil causes the armature to act as a magnet. The armature poles are attracted to field poles having the opposite polarity, causing the armature to rotate.
2. The commutator reverses the armature current at the moment when unlike poles of the armature and field are facing each other, reversing the polarity of the armature field. Like poles of the armature and field then *repel* each other, causing continuous rotation of the armature in the same direction.

## MOTOR MAINTENANCE

The biggest maintenance problem with DC motors is brush wear. The brushes are held against the commutator with light spring tension. In time they wear down, changing their shape and close fit to the commutator. The commutator will likely roughen and begin arcing, too. Better motors will have easy access to the brush holders from outside the motor housing (usually under plastic screw caps) near one end of the motor. If not, the case may have to be disassembled to get at them. Replacement brushes are usually available at electric supply houses. If the commutator is rough, it should be smoothed with fine sandpaper (never emery cloth) when the brushes are replaced. New brushes should be fitted to the commutator by wrapping a strip of sandpaper around the commutator, sand side up, and turning the armature back and forth while holding the brush, in its holder, lightly against the sandpaper. A few strokes should make it conform to the commutator shape. *Don't overdo it!*

Bearings and lubrication make up the rest of the normal motor maintenance problems. And lack of lubrication is responsible for most bearing problems. Some motors have oiler holes with snap-close lids on them, but not all are so fitted. The armature is supported by end bearings. Inexpensive motors designed for intermittent use have cheaper sleeve bearings (called friction bearings), which depend upon a film of oil to separate the parts. Heavy-duty motors use anti-friction bearings such as ball bearings for support. Some friction bearings are called "self-lubricating" or "permanent" bearings because they are formed from oil-impregnated powdered metal. In electric motors, too much oil or grease can be nearly as bad as too little, so don't over-lubricate them! If you can hear a motor running, it is calling for some attention. Noise is the first sign of dry bearings. If neglected, the hum will become a whine and over-heating will begin, soon to be followed by expansion of parts, binding and finally failure. Some marine motors are completely sealed, so there is little that can be done to them. If they start to get noisy, a shot of penetrating oil, applied where the shaft comes through the housing, may quiet them down for a while.

### STARTER MOTORS

The starter is the biggest motor, in terms of current demand, that you have on board. It has its own, unfused, circuit, which we have already talked about several times. Another high-current motor, second only to the starter in demand, is an anchor windlass or capstan, mounted on the foredeck. These battery-killers draw at least 20 amps, depending on the line pull and speed at which they run, and can draw considerably more. I would *never* consider using one on a boat whose only electrical system was 12-volt. The foredeck is as far as you can get from your battery. When you check the table of wire size for the maximum current and that length, you're looking at an expensive installation. If you are considering one of these because your health and strength are not what they used to be, first determine the mechanical advantage of a manual windlass with a long handle, and then compare the two pulls. You'll be amazed how much a long handle lever can do for you, and it will work even when the batteries are dead.

Sometimes a motor will be rated in terms of "fractional horse-power" rather than watts on the label or spec sheet. How much current will it draw then? One horsepower is equal to 746 watts, but that assumes the motor can convert the energy at 100% efficiency. Of course, it cannot. Considering all the possible energy losses, you should at least double that value to 1500 watts per hp. Some experts recommend using 1800 watts per hp. for DC motors. This allows for the initial surge of current that occurs when the motor first starts. So if you have a $1/25$ hp. motor, multiply by 1500 watts per hp. and you'll get 60 watts as the equivalent power rating at 50% efficiency. Then

$I = P/V$ so the current will be 60 watts divided by 12 volts, or 5 amps. If you had used 1800 watts, your answer would be 6 amps.

## REFRIGERATOR MOTORS

Another fairly high current demand motor is found in electric refrigerator compressors. You have to wire for the maximum current, but when you estimate amp-hours, remember that the device does not run all the time. How often it is on depends more on the amount and quality of the box insulation, how many times you open the door a day, how often you remove ice cubes, and what you put in it. A power boat or a motorsailer might consider an engine-driven compressor, rather than an electric unit. But many auxiliary sailboats are already underpowered and cannot afford to pull any more horsepower from the engine. Their other choice is a solid-state or "thermoelectric" unit. These units depend on a peculiar effect—discovered more than 150 years ago by the French physicist J. C. A. Peltier. In the device the passage of current causes cooling in a specially-devised semi-conductor. There are no moving parts in the cooling system. In most thermoelectrics, a small fan is the only moving part. Low power consumption is advertised, but check the specifications carefully before you buy one. Better yet, talk to a satisfied owner.

## BILGE PUMPS

Your bilge pump is another motor-driven device. Most are wired with a three-position switch: ON-OFF-AUTOMATIC. Off and on let you manually control the pump. That's fine when you are aboard, but when the boat is unattended you can leave the switch in the automatic position. Then the pump will be actuated by a float switch that turns it on when the water level lifts the float to its ON position. When enough water has been pumped overboard, the float drops to OFF and shuts down the pump. That's when they work properly. Certain float switches have been known to hang up and not shut off. The motor continues to run until the batteries are discharged. The boat can then fill with water and sink.

Older wooden boats are most susceptible to this unfortunate event, often at their mooring or slip, but even fiberglass and steel vessels are not immune. Their problem is more often a leaking stuffing box or through-hull fitting. Bilge pumps often are selected on price rather than volume or "head." Head refers to how high the pump will lift the water to discharge it. Volume is how many gallons per hour or per minute the pump is capable of delivering on a sustained basis. And the two terms are interrelated. That's why you cannot always assume that the pump will deliver, on your boat, the volume stated on the label or in the catalog. If you lift the water higher, the volume delivered will decrease. A bilge pump on a power boat will seldom have to lift water more than a couple of feet to discharge it above the waterline. But on a deep-keeled cruising sailboat, the same pump might have to lift the water 4 or 5 feet—with a significant decrease in gallons per hour (GPH) evacuated.

Let's look at some numbers. A quick perusal of electric bilge pump listings in some recent catalogs reveals a whole spectrum of sizes ranging from a low of 222 gallons per hour (list price $86.95) to a high of 3500 gallons per hour—"highest capacity submersible bilge pump available"—which lists at $104. One 1200 GPH model is billed "High Capacity." It is often difficult to cut through the advertisers' hype to find the truth. *None* of these catalog listings mentioned the head used to rate the maximum pump output, except for one manufacturer who referred to "open flow," which appears to mean zero head. Only *one* manufacturer (the same one) gave any rating data at all, for two models:

| "2000 MODEL" | "1300 MODEL" |
|:---:|:---:|
| 1800 GPH at 2' head | 1300 GPH open flow |
| 1560 GPH at 4' head | 800 GPH at 3' head |
| 1412 GPH at 6' head | 500 GPH at 8' head |

How do we compare all these numbers? Well, we might start by noting that an ordinary kitchen faucet may deliver 6 to 8 gallons per minute, or about 360 gallons per hour, which doesn't sound like much. But that is more than six 55-gallon drums full. And a faucet-size leak is *nothing* compared with a hull holed below the waterline. Dan Spurr, in *Upgrading the*

*Cruising Sailboat,* points out, that a 1½-inch hole two feet below the waterline admits 71 gallons of water per minute, or *4260 gallons per hour!* That exceeds the output of the largest available electric bilge pump operating with little or no head and a fully charged battery. Does that give you some pause? It should.

Fiberglass and steel boats have such little normal water seepage there is a tendency to believe all you need is a small-volume pump. But you don't buy a bilge pump for seepage, you buy one for *survival!* When you hit a log or rock, lose a seacock, or rupture a hose on an engine cooling water line, that's when you need high-volume water evacuation. However, you'll pay more for a pump that can deliver, and the current drain will be considerably higher (up to 15 amps). There's no free lunch anywhere.

There is a trade-off that makes more sense to me than buying a vastly oversized electric bilge pump for your boat. That is to carry an oversized *manual* pump. Not a dinky little plastic toy, but rather something like a gallon-per-stroke or a 30-gallons-per-minute diaphragm pump. Use the modest electric pump for normal seepage, but keep the survival hand pump where you can get to it in a hurry. It will keep on pumping when your batteries are submerged—just as long as you can keep on stroking.

All gasoline-engine powered vessels built after August 1, 1980, as well as those having permanently installed gasoline electric generators or donkey engines for mechanical power (like pot haulers on a fishing boat) must ventilate the engine compartment with a power blower—unless the compartment is open to the atmosphere. Of course, the blower's electric motor must be "ignition protected." Here's another place where, if you must replace a defective or burned-out blower unit, you can't just buy the cheapest one in the store. The replacement must be of the same rated air flow as the original. The boat builder had to choose a blower that would completely change the air in the engine compartment, plus all other compartments that open to it, every minute. Make sure the replacement will do it, too.

Other motors can be found in air-horn compressors, windshield wipers, electric sheet and halyard winches, and ventila-

**Figure 6–6:**
*Oscillating cabin fan stirs the air with only 1.2 amp drain. (Courtesy of The Guest Corporation.)*

tion fans. While boats that cruise south of Chesapeake Bay already know about using wind scoops for pushing air through the interior, there are always those hot, muggy, deathly still nights when a cabin fan will pay for itself in comfort. Make sure you get one that won't kill your batteries, though.

## ELECTRONICS

Are you dismayed by the plethora of electronic devices that confront you at every boat show and adorn the pages of boating magazines and catalogs? Fifteen years ago not many cruising boats had a radio. Now weekenders are adding lorans. Prices continue to tumble while the devices get more reliable and complex. We are all caught up in the high-technology revolution and no one seems to have any idea where it will take us. Who can say what is essential and what is gimmickry? I'm not going to get rid of my sextant, but the next time I move aboard for more than a summer cruise my computer and word processor will go with me. That's how quickly we adapt to changing times. Today I found in my mailbox a magazine with a full-page ad for a new marine computer whose 10 functions of speed, time and distance completely eclipse my old taffrail log; and it sells for only $250.

A VHF-FM radio is an essential item aboard every cruising boat, for both safety and survival. Beyond that, my only advice for electronics is to refer back to the list of questions I gave you earlier this chapter. Installation of some sensitive electronic devices, such as loran and satnav, demand they be connected directly to the battery, rather than being wired through the control panel—to cut down on interference. Several such hook-ups could lead to a rats nest of wires right at the battery terminals. A new "battery jack" attaches to each battery terminal wing-nut stud and provides places for four direct connections. As we mentioned earlier, most electronic devices have their own internal fuses, or else a line fuse in the positive power wire.

Many navigational electronic devices available today: loran, satnav, radio direction finders (both hand-held and add-on VHF units), combination loran/satnav, Omega, radar, depth sounders, radio weather facsimile chart recorders, SSB radio, CB radio, ham radio, and autopilots. There also are recreational electronics that we might wish to consider, such as AM-FM stereo, tape deck and TV. Expensive marine stereo units can be found, but I find that a good auto radio with tape deck works fine.

## INSTALLATION

The great majority of all today's marine electronic equipment can be installed by the owner. This is a far cry from just a few years ago when radars had complicated fixed-wave guides connecting the antenna to the receiver, when loran-As were so temperamental they would sometimes not work when the engine was running and in certain weather conditions, and when the quality of the old AM radio communication was so poor most cruisers did not bother to install one.

But just because you CAN install your own, should you? That depends upon you and your capabilities. If you built your own boat, there is little you can't do. So I'd say go ahead. You already have demonstrated superior technical ability. If you bought the boat off the shelf, so to speak, and have little experience with electronics, then you'd better leave the installation details to an experienced technician. But if you have installed a CB radio or an AM-FM tape deck in your automobile, you certainly should be able to put one on your boat, too, as well as other similar radio receivers, including loran, satnav, etc. They are really no big deal, as long as you follow the installation instructions very carefully.

I would recommend leaving installation of radar and SSB radio transmitters to the experts, although they can be bought from mail-order catalogs for owner-installation. A word to the wise here. Not all mail-order houses are factory-authorized dealers for all the electronic brands they sell. An extremely low price may not turn out to be such a bargain if you are unable to make a claim under warranty. There is a lot to be said for supporting your local marine electronics shops. Their prices may run a little higher (they have sales, too—usually around boat show time), but they will be there to service the equipment when you need them.

## POWER CONSUMPTION

Today's electronics are exclusively solid-state, which means very low power consumption. Sailboats that make extended passages might be concerned with the difference between an 8 watt (¾ amp) navigation receiver and one rated at 15 watts (1-¼ amp). If it runs for several weeks at a time, that can make a difference in the total amp-hours taken out of the batteries. But for most powerboats and coastal cruisers, the difference is insignificant. The only high-drain devices are radio transmitters, but only while they are transmitting (radar is a transmitter, too). A VHF-FM will receive with less than one amp of current, but requires 5 to 6 amps to transmit. The VHF-FM transmitter is limited to 25 watts of output power, but you have to put in 60 to 70 watts to get it. Single sideband (or SSB) radios put out up to 150 watts of radiated power, so they have to draw about as much current as an anchor windlass while transmitting—20 to 30 amps! Radars may be rated at several kilowatts of radiated power, but they fire their energy in such short bursts that current drain is only 5 amps or less for today's models. But you have to consider the total current drain for each and every item that you add to your system—and be sure to make the calculation before you make the purchase.

## INTERFERENCE

RFI, or radio frequency interference, can be a problem for some radio receivers and depth sounders. We ran into it already when we were looking at fluorescent lights, remember? Actually, according to Skipper Marine Electronics' *1984 Miscellaneous Marine Electronics Instruments Buyers Guide,* "Anything that consumes or creates electricity (12VDC or 110VAC) can cause interference. Typical causes of interference are on-board TV sets, lights, alternators, bilge pumps, tachometers, windshield wiper motors, etc." This free booklet includes the best table I know of detailing possible electronic interference problems (or noise), their probable sources, the proper filters to eliminate each problem, and where to install each filter. Skipper's filter prices run from $12.95 to $79. In other catalogs you can find alternator noise suppressor filters for as little as $6 and antenna noise filters (VHF-FM, ham, and CB) for under $15. But don't worry about getting filters unless you find that you really need them. Most new electronic equipment is so good they seldom are necessary anymore. Where my old loran-A was a nightmare. The loran-C that replaced it is a jewel. It has no external line filters, and the antenna is attached to the dinghy davits at a 30° angle with the horizontal. From my mooring in Rhode Island I can lock in on the Northeast US chain, the Southeast US chain, and the Great Lakes chain—it will pick up the North Atlantic chain, but won't lock on it.

If you do find you have a noise or interference problem turn off all the electrical systems and the engine. Turn on the receiver that picks up the interference (loran or radio, usually) and let it warm up. Start the engine and check for ignition noise (if gasoline; diesels won't have any). Turn on the alternator and check again for a whine in the radio that changes frequency with engine speed, or a loran that loses its lines of position. If the problem hasn't shown up yet, then turn on each electrical device, one at a time, and check for interference until you have located the culprit. The inexpensive remedy is not to use the two items at the same time. If that's not practical, get a proper filter and install it in the power leads of the noise source.

These are some of the things that come on when you turn the switch. No list could possibly be all-inclusive. By the time this book gets into print, new ones will be on the market. How many of them you will need, or want, depends entirely on you and your crew. Just beware the proliferation of non-essential items.

**Figure 6–7:** *Complete wiring diagram for a typical single engine cruising boat. Can you follow your way through each of these circuits?*

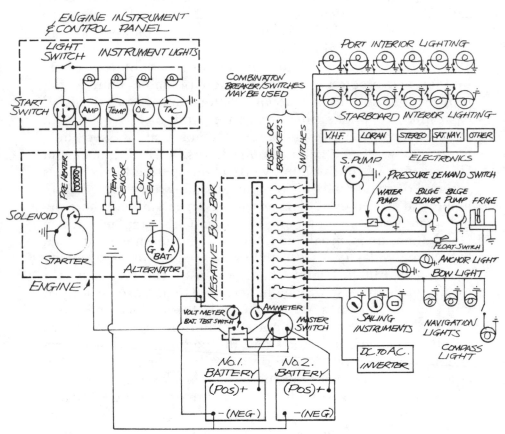

## Chapter 7

# RECHARGING THE BATTERY

## MULTIPLE BATTERY ISOLATORS

Before we begin discussing charging the batteries, we first should look at a common problem of all multiple battery or battery bank installations. We talked about these banks earlier, and we also looked at how they can be controlled manually with a battery selector switch. Depending upon the situation, we can choose Battery 1, or Battery 2, or Both, which puts them together in parallel. If the batteries are in good shape, and they are being actively charged, then we can direct the charge to either Number 1, Number 2, or to Both at the same time. If one battery is more discharged than the other, it will receive more of the charging current than the one with higher charge when in the Both position, and the two batteries will eventually become fully charged. No problem exists as long as a charging current, either from the engine-driven charger or from some other source is being supplied, and you remember to move the switch to the proper settings for charge and discharge. If you forget to do this, there may be a problem. If you leave the switch in the Both position when not charging, the battery with higher charge (and voltage) will discharge into the lower one; eventually both batteries will come to equal voltages and states of charge. You may end up with two nearly discharged batteries instead of one good one and one low one. The worst-case scenario is losing your starting battery while you are anchored in some beautiful isolated cove on an uninhabited island, you know how Murphy's Laws work. No sweat, you say? Just give a holler on Channel 16. You can holler in the microphone all you want, but with dead or even low batteries, nobody's going to hear you. What to do? Don't let it happen; install a *battery isolator.* This is a device that contains solid-state diodes, which allow current to pass in only one direction—electrical check valves. The charging output goes to the isolator, which in turn directs the current to each battery, independently of the other. Both batteries are always being charged automatically whenever the engine is running, and one cannot discharge into the other. It's a simple solution to a vexing problem. Here is what one looks like. Later we'll see how one is wired into the total circuit.

**Figure 7–1:** *Diodes in the battery isolator direct the charging current to both batteries and prevent one from discharging into the other. (Courtesy of The Guest Corporation.)*

L 4½", W 3¼", H 3¼"

L 6½", W 4½", H 3¼"

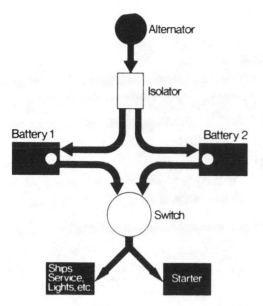

**Figure 7–2:** *Battery isolator schematic. (Courtesy of The Guest Corporation.)*

## ALTERNATORS AND GENERATORS

Practically all boats with inboard engines—and some outboard powered ones—generate electricity for battery charging whenever the engine is running. Newly-built boats, or ones that have had a recent engine replacement, will most likely use an alternator for charging. Older boats and engines, a few new diesels and some new imported engines, will still be using generators, just as in older cars. But generators are not passé. They are heavy, rugged, can survive more abuse than alternators, and will be found on boats for a long time to come. For all practical purposes, they both do the same job. They take some of the mechanical energy produced by the engine and convert it into electrical energy. Alternators just do it a little better. Both devices produce an alternating current in their windings, and in both cases this is changed into direct current before it leaves the unit. How they do this is different. There is little that we, as average boat owners, can do about investigating or repairing the insides of either of these devices—except for cleaning the commutator and replacing the brushes on a generator. So I won't bore you with all the intricacies of internal

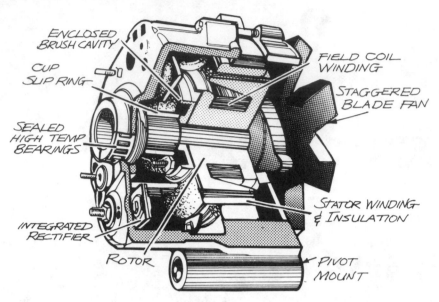

**Figure 7–3:** *Alternator design features.*

construction features of either. I'll just say that alternators have become so popular in recent years because they are lighter, they rotate at higher speeds without flying apart (they can turn at higher engine speed ratios and have more output at idle r.p.m.), and they do not arc and spark at their brushes like generators.

We should pause here a moment to define or recheck the meanings of some terms. Some we have run into before, but in a different context.

**Brushes** are carbon blocks that wipe against the commutator or slip rings to complete the electrical connection to the rotating coil.

**Commutator** is a segmentated rotary switch through which the electrical connections are made to the rotating coil of a DC generator or motor. It automatically reverses the current going into or out of the coil at the appropriate time.

**Diode** is a two-element semi-conductor device that allows current to pass only one way.

**Poles** refer to magnetic poles, north and south. A two-pole generator has one pair of poles, one north and one south. A multi-pole alternator has more than one pair of poles.

**Rectifier** uses a commutator (on generators) or diodes on alternators to convert AC to DC.

**Regulator** is a device that controls the output of a generator or alternator.

**Rotor** is a rotating coil. We called it an armature in a DC motor. It is the field coil in an alternator.

**Slip rings** are continuous, non-segmented, rotary switches used to make electrical connections to the rotating coil of an AC generator and some AC motors.

**Stator** refers to the stationary coils and poles in a motor or generator. The stator is attached to the housing.

The Battery Council International identifies and lists 6 main differences between alternators and DC generators in its Battery Service Manual. They are:

1. Rectification on DC generators is accomplished by use of a commutator. On the alternator this is accomplished by use of diodes.
2. Field and armature are transposed in the generator and alternator. The field rotates on the alternator while the field is stationary on the generator. Conversely, the armature rotates on the generator while it is stationary on the alternator.
3. Brushes carry full load current on the generator, but only field current on the alternator.
4. The alternator weighs considerably less than the generator, due mainly to eliminating the heavy frame necessary on generators.
5. Alternators are multi-pole, while the standard automotive generators are two-pole.
6. Control systems for the alternator differ somewhat from those of the generators. Each system will be explained in the service manual supplied by the alternator's manufacturer.

## THE REGULATOR

With a generator, the regulator always is found in a separate "black box." When the lid is opened, you will see three separate units inside:

1. Reverse current relay or cutout, which stops current from flowing back from the battery to the generator when it is not charging and "motorizing" the generator.
2. Voltage regulator, which controls the output voltage of the generator by regulating the field current. This prevents destroying the battery by overcharging.
3. Current limiter, this protects the generator from excessive output and overheating by limiting the output current to its maximum designed safe value.

## MAKING ADJUSTMENTS

Each unit has a set of contacts or points, which are closed by electromagnetic pull, and opened by spring tension. Adjustments are usually possible by turning some screws to change the spring tensions. But if you don't know exactly what you are doing, LEAVE THEM ALONE! When you feel that you are ready to tackle a more challenging job like that, look for one of the more advanced books on the market, such as *Your Boat's Electrical System* by Miller and Maloney, or *The 12 Volt Doctor's Practical Handbook* by Ed Beyn. The latter book includes some interesting projects for expanding, updating and improving your boat's electrical system, including good winter projects for the off-season.

Alternators use a much simpler regulator system than generators. One brand may look quite different from another. Some are located in a separate box, while others are built right into the alternator housing. An alternator is self-limiting in its current output, so it doesn't need a current regulator. The diodes used for rectification (change of AC to DC) also prevent back flow of current from the battery to the alternator. All that is left is to regulate the output voltage to protect the battery and other components. This is accomplished by turning the field current in the rotor off and on to maintain a constant output voltage. Earlier alternator regulators contain a single electromagnetic switch in which a movable contact oscillates between two fixed points. One energizes the field, the other grounds it. Newer regulator models rely more on solid-state electronics to perform the switching function instead of points and springs. Diodes and transistors can sense the field current and switch it in an extremely quick and efficient manner. These units can be miniaturized and "potted" (sealed in plastic). Some regulators are temperature-compensated with a thermistor, a device that changes resistance with temperature changes, so that the alternator output will better match the charge-acceptance characteristics of the battery, which vary with the temperature of the battery. The voltage is decreased for high temperatures and increased for low ones, all automatically.

## CHECKING CHARGING VOLTAGE

What about the charging voltage? Why is it that if the battery is fully charged at 12.6 volts, the panel voltmeter will read nearly 15 volts when the engine is running? The battery charging voltage is the voltage measured across the battery when it is being charged by the alternator or generator. It consists of two parts, and is equal to their sum:

1. The battery voltage.
2. The voltage drop across the battery's internal resistance.

Back in Chapter 2 we said we'd return to internal resistance of batteries later; that's now. This internal resistance or source resistance opposes the flow of current into the battery to recharge it, and also out of the battery when we are using it. When we measure battery voltage with a meter, either a portable meter with the probes directly on the terminals, or by looking at the panel meter, we read the open-circuit voltage; no load current is flowing, just the small amount required to make the meter work. You can get a voltage reading on open-circuit that indicates a good state of battery charge, but still is not able to start the engine because the internal resistance is too high, impeding the flow of current. In order to see what a battery is capable of delivering, we must evaluate it under load conditions. The biggest load is the starter, so that's why it is usually used for this test.

According to Ohm's Law, if we measure the short circuit or no-load current through an ammeter and divide it into the open-circuit voltage, we should get the internal resistance. That's true, because it is the only resistance in the circuit acting to limit the current. But it's not usually done that way. (It may even be dangerous.) Here's one way to do it with just a volt-meter. First, check the open-circuit voltage to be sure the battery is charged. Second, have someone crank the engine for 15 seconds *without starting* while you watch the voltmeter. For average boating season temperatures (50° to 70°F) the meter should read 9.5 volts or more after cranking. If it is much lower than that, you're probably in need of a new battery. This is a quick-and-dirty check. But before you pull out your credit card or checkbook to buy a new battery, have the battery store or marina shop give it a proper load test with an adjustable load tester to verify the results. Batteries can be properly evaluated only under load, because, remember, it is their internal resistance that determines how much they can deliver to that load.

The output voltage from the alternator must be large enough to overcome the battery voltage plus the voltage drop across its internal resistance in order to push charges into the battery and cause the battery-charging chemical reactions to take place. That's why the charging voltage must always be higher than the battery voltage. The internal resistance is temporarily increased when gassing occurs and a film of bubbles coats the plates. As the gases dissipate, the resistance will decrease. Sulfated plates that have become hard and crystallized will have a permanently higher internal resistance, usually caused by using the battery in a constant state of discharge—too low a regulator setting or too much load on the battery. Other factors that will affect the charging voltage are temperature, electrolyte concentration, plate area contacting the electrolyte, battery age, and electrolyte impurities (do you use hard mineral water to fill the battery?).

### REGULATOR SETTINGS

Most voltage regulators are set at just over 14 volts. The following recommendations were obtained from a Surrette official. The best all-around setting is 14.2 volts. On a motoryacht, 14.2 volts should keep your batteries in good shape, because they will be charging whenever the vessel is underway—which is not all the time for a pleasure boat. A sailing auxiliary, which uses the engine only for short periods of time—and then only occasionally—might not be able to keep the batteries topped off with this setting. It may be necessary to increase the regulator setting up to as much as 14.5 volts, but then you're stuck with a value that could overcharge the batteries if you have to power all day sometime. Workboats sometimes set their regulators below 14 volts, because their engines ARE running all the time. If the batteries get hot while charging, the rate is too high. Beware, and do something about it. Spa Creek Instrument Company sells a manual alternator control that allows you to regulate the output to match the way you are using your boat —high charge rate for short runs, and lower rate for extended powering. This is an ideal solution if you like to control your own destiny rather than relying on complete automation. But it's not so good if you tend to be forgetful about such things. Overcharging will send you to the battery store quicker than undercharging will. One of the *The 12 Volt Doctor's Handbook* projects is building your own manual control; that alone is worth the price of the book, in case you are interested.

## RECHARGE RATES

One thing we never see, unless we have a system ammeter installed (most boats don't) is just how the alternator actually recharges the batteries. Say your alternator is rated at 60 amps. When you run the engine for one hour, won't the battery receive 60 amp-hours of charge? No, no, no. It doesn't work that way. No alternator can deliver its rated current for any length of time without overheating. Figure about half of rated value for sustained output. That brings us down to 30 amps, but we can't even get that for an hour straight with a standard regulator. The regulator gives a constant voltage, not a constant current. When the battery is low, we'll get more current to charge it— but not for very long. According to Battery Council International (BCI) data, a regulator set at 14.4 volts will deliver an initial 30 amps to a half-charged 12-volt battery, but only 14 amps to one with three-quarter charge, and a measly 2 amps to a fully-charged battery. We see this same situation on our automobile. Right after starting, the ammeter needle swings over to the right for a little while, but soon drifts back to near center. That's why, when we inadvertently leave a light on all day and deep cycle our battery, it takes so long to get it recharged again.

Also, the recharge rate is extremely temperature-sensitive. On a cold winter day when the battery temperature is 0° F (−17.8° C) the half-charged battery we mentioned earlier, the one that should be able to accept 30 amps of charging current, will actually accept only 2 amps! But at 80° F (26.7° C), it will take 27 amps, nearly all it is capable of accepting. At 120° F, not too difficult to obtain inside a hot engine room, the battery will take the full output of the alternator or generator. That's when overcharging can be a real threat to your electrical system. Regulating the charging current is no simple task. BCI defines the ideal voltage setting for a regulator as "that setting which will keep the battery at or near full charge with a minimum use of water when the vehicle is used in its customary way." Substitute boat for vehicle and it still applies. If the battery uses more than two ounces (30-60 ml) of water each 25 hours of engine time, the regulator needs resetting. Keep a careful record of battery service and you'll have fewer unexpected problems.

Now let's look beyond the self-contained engine-driven charging system for a while. Many times we will not want to run the engine just to recharge the batteries. It's an expensive way to get electricity. It's also noisy and often inconvenient. What are our other options? Let's see.

## AC SHORE POWER AND SOLID-STATE CHARGER

The yellow umbilical cord is the answer when you are tied to the shore. Whether it's metered or a fee is added to your daily or monthly bill, it usually is cheaper to buy your electricity this way than to burn fuel to make it. Harvey Hubbell, Inc. is one leading U.S. manufacturer of these ship-to-shore electrical connectors, or as they like to refer to them, "dockside life support systems."

Once shore power in the form of 125-volt AC comes aboard, there may be a tendency to want to wire the whole boat with a complex dual-power system. Such a setup is beyond the scope of this book; that's why we put 12-Volt DC in the title. If your boat came with such a system, fine. But installing one presents many more problems than most boat owners are apt to be able

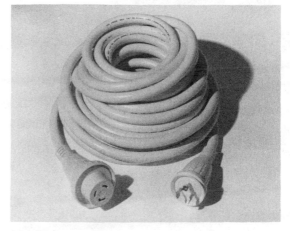

**Figure 7–4:** *Dockside power cable rated for 30 amps at 125 volts AC. (Courtesy of Harvey Hubbell, Inc.)*

to handle. The potential hazards are real and the consequences of not doing the job right can be lethal. If you want to use household appliances on your boat while at the dock, hire a professional to install them properly. Don't try to hook them up with a rat's nest of cheap extension cords and octopus plugs.

When we refer to shore power AC, we assume it is being delivered to a device that is converting or rectifying it into DC at 12 volts. This current then charges the boat's batteries to supply all electrical needs while tied to the shore. Raritan Engineering Company, Inc. calls its units "Crown II Converters," Ray Jefferson's devices are Battery Guard or Switcher Battery Charger, and The Guest Corporation calls its units Battery Chargers/Converters. One word of warning. If you are going to go this route, do it right. Don't just pick up a $15 battery charger on sale at your local discount automotive store and plug it into a dock outlet with a couple of 12-foot lamp-wire extension cords. Somebody's apt to get killed that way. Don't let it be you.

A Hubbell article, "Maintaining Your Boat's Dockside Power System" contains some excellent advice to users of these power cables.

1. Turn OFF boat's main shore power switch and disconnect cable set from power source before performing any maintenance on these items.

**Figure 7–5:** *Raritan Crown automatic marine converter, 30-amp model.*

**Figure 7–6:** *Ray Jefferson regulated DC battery guard, 15-amp model.*

**Figure 7–7:** *Guest automatic marine battery chargers, 15-amp and 40-amp models. (Note the differences in size among the various units.)*

2. Periodically rinse exposed metal parts in clean fresh water, dry completely, and spray with moisture repellant; especially if dropped into or splashed with salt water.
3. Periodically check exposed contacts for "pitting" and burn or "flash" marks or signs of deterioration or discoloration of the plastic. They indicate poor contact or high resistance connections—the devices should be replaced.
4. Check for a bad receptacle by feeling the plug 15 minutes and again one hour after hook-up. If it is uncomfortably warm, you have a bad connection. Contact dockmaster.
5. If connectors have been abused (dropped, stepped on, or run over) make sure the contacts are realigned before trying to reconnect them.
6. Keep the cable clean and wipe with a vinyl protector.
7. Avoid "Bad Plug/Bad Receptacle Syndrome." A good cable or receptacle can be ruined by mating it with a bad one. Both devices must then be replaced at the same time, or the process will be repeated.

## PROPER AC CONVERTER/CHARGERS

The differences between a proper boat AC converter/battery charger and a discount automotive model are many, but two are of paramount importance:

1. Electrical isolation between the 120-volt AC circuit and the battery circuit.
2. Non-trickle type charge delivery.

American Boat and Yacht Council standards require all transformers used in marine battery chargers to be of the isolation type. The two coils, primary (120 volts) and secondary (12 volts), are connected only magnetically, not electrically. We first met the transformer back in Chapter 2. Depicted here is a step-down transformer in a marine battery charger. The iron core makes the magnetic coupling more efficiently. That's because it is easier for the magnetic field to pass through the iron than the surrounding air. There is no electrical connection between the coils. Less expensive models sometimes use an auto-transformer, whose windings are NOT electrically independent of each other. In fact, they may be the same coil with

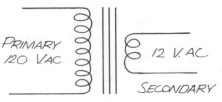

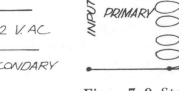

**Figure 7–8:** *Step down transformer.*

**Figure 7–9:** *Step down autotransformer.*

different taps, as shown here. The coil usually is wrapped around an iron core, often ring-shaped. Variable output can be obtained if a sliding tap is used. Then the unit is commonly known by its trade name "Powerstat" or "Variac." If the two circuits are not isolated, there is a very real danger of introducing stray currents aboard your boat—strong stray currents that pose a shock hazard and threaten to set up corroding stray currents in the water around your boat.

If you have a 12-volt test lamp, here's a quick way to check for isolation of a battery charger. If you don't, look ahead to the next chapter, "Troubleshooting The System," where you'll learn how to make one. Set your charger near a metal water pipe. Hook one of the battery clips to one test lamp wire and touch the other lamp wire to the water pipe when the charger is turned on. It should not light. Reverse the charger power plug and try again. Hook the lamp to the other battery clip and perform both tests again. The lamp should never light. If it does, it indicates some electrical connection between the 120-volt AC circuit and the 12-volt DC circuit, usually through a common ground.

Trickle chargers are not desirable in steady use on your boat. Even though they put out less than an amp, there is a danger that continuous overcharging for an indefinite length of time will destroy the grids of the batteries' positive plates. Marine chargers automatically turn themselves off when the batteries are fully charged to avoid overcharge. When the battery energy level drops, the charger senses it and automatically turns itself on to restore full charge. Here is a wiring diagram for a complete charging system, as we have described it so far.

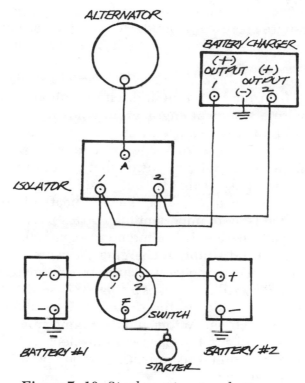

**Figure 7–10:** *Single engine, two-battery installation with battery charger and isolator.*

## DANGER: SHOCK AND ELECTROLYSIS

Since this is the only time AC shore power is discussed in this book, two other items must be mentioned before continuing. These are the shore grounding wire and ground fault circuit interrupters (GFCI).

The shore grounding wire—and how properly to use it—has probably been debated by boatyard and marina sages as much as any other single topic. In fact, while I was writing this section two items appeared in boating magazines dealing directly with the topic. One was a letter, in which the writer described the shorting out of a dockside electrical outlet during a storm, and the subsequent melting of a wire-reinforced hose between his boat's hot water heater and the engine. The writer believed the problem was caused by a short from one of the power leads to the third-wire electrical ground. He stated it was not customary to ground this wire on a boat because of stray currents and electrolysis.

That same month another magazine article dealt with the controversy over the green ground wire for shore power. The author, a marine electrical engineer, unequivocally stated that the shore grounding wire must always be connected to the boat ground, in accordance with recognized safety standards. He realized the problems with corrosion that grounding it may introduce, but pointed out that by not grounding, one increases the chance of electrocution, either on your boat or in the water. Human survival is more important than boat survival.

There is an alternative. If you intend to expand the use of AC on your boat beyond simply recharging the batteries, I highly recommend you use a special isolation transformer circuit for it, as prescribed by ABYC. This is a single-phase, 1:1 ratio (neither step-up nor step-down) transformer that completely separates the shore electrical system and its ground from the boat's. This system eliminates the danger from electrical shock and from galvanic corrosion. It is especially important to use such a system on a metal boat.

Now that was easy for me to say. The ABYC recommendation for AC isolation makes such eminent good sense that no one can argue against it—it's like God, motherhood and the flag. But very few boatbuilders are using it. I checked with a couple of builders of large semi-custom fiberglass sailing yachts and found they never had installed one, even as an option. In talking with their engineers, I found why. The three key words in describing an isolation transformer are: big, heavy, expensive. Because of their weight, they should be installed low in the boat; but that's where they are most subject to rust and corrosion, just what you don't need for a device you are installing to protect you. Besides, they are hard to find. You won't find them listed in marine catalogs (I looked), nor stocked by marine stores, chandleries or marine electronics shops (I tried), nor carried by major marine electronics dealers. If you decide to go this route, despite the weight and expense, try a major electrical supply house in your nearest big city—that's where I finally found them. I don't mean this to sound so negative. I'm merely reporting there is a considerable gap between "official recommendations" and "actual practice." However, when I get around to building my steel retirement boat, I *will* find a place for the isolation transformer. I am convinced they are not only worthwhile, but necessary.

Another device that should be used whenever 120-volt AC is brought aboard a boat, even if it is just temporarily by means of an extension cord at a dock to power an electric hand drill or a saw for some minor modification, is a ground fault circuit interrupter (GFCI). Hubbell makes both built-in receptacles with GFCI and portable units in several sizes. (Many, many other GFCI receptacles are on the market, but Hubbell and a few others pay special attention to insulation materials and design.) Those boat builders and engineers I talked with about isolation transformers did tell me that they *are* using GFCIs on their boats. Some use GFCIs on individual outlets in the head and galley, and some use full-circuit protection.

**Figure 7–11:** *Ground fault circuit interrupter flush-mounted receptacle for on-board AC plug ins. (Courtesy of Harvey Hubbell, Inc.)*

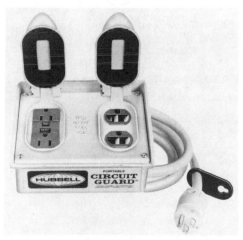

**Figure 7–12:** *Portable ground fault circuit interrupter protects as many as four tools at the same time.*

Hubbell's catalog describes these devices and provides some good insight into how they operate and what they will and will not do. They are so succinct that, with Hubbell's permission, I'll just quote them.

"While conventional 3-wire grounding is essential to electrical safety on board any boat, it cannot protect against minute line-to-ground faults that cannot activate protective devices such as fuses or circuit breakers. Conventional overcurrent protection begins at 15 amperes. The fuse will blow or the breaker will open only if the current exceeds its rating. Contrary to popular belief, current values of less than $\frac{1}{10}$ of one ampere passing through the human body can be very harmful. A Ground Fault Circuit Interrupter (GFCI) senses any ground fault larger than $\frac{6}{1000}$ of an ampere and shuts off the power before an accident can happen. These units are available for use with power tools or other electrical equipment on the boat or dock, The units require 120-volt circuits and must be used in addition to fuses and circuit breakers—not instead of them—and GFCI must be used only on a grounded system, even though the grounding wire is not used in the operation of the device."

"Circuit Guard Receptacles are designed to provide protection against electrical shock hazards due to line-to-ground faults. Although the Circuit Guard Receptacle does not limit the magnitude of the fault current, and therefore cannot prevent electric shock, it does limit the duration of the shock to a period considered safe for normally healthy persons. Circuit Guard Receptacles will provide protection against ground faults only. They will not protect against overloads or short circuits. There is no known device that will guard against the electrical shock hazard resulting from contact with both the 'hot' and neutral wires of the electric circuit."

## MAINTAINING PROPER POLARITY

In AC circuits the two conductors are the black and white wires. The "hot" wire referred to is the *black* one. The white wire is neutral, which is supposed to be grounded on shore, but *never on the boat*. Green is used for the grounding wire, but it is never wired into a circuit—only to the metallic frame or case of every single electrical device. It is there to protect the user in case a fault ever develops between the hot wire and the case, to shunt the fault current off directly to ground, rather than through the user. *The green wire is never switched or fused.*

When someone speaks about maintaining proper AC polarity or avoiding reverse polarity, he refers to the black and white wires. The black wire must always be hot and the white wire neutral, and they must never be interchanged, neither on the boat nor in the shore circuit—whether knowingly or inadvertently. You may know what you are doing on your boat, but the marina may have had some unskilled workers hooking things up who didn't know that it made a difference which wire went where—"AC goes both ways, doesn't it?". That kind of thinking can lead to the neutral wire becoming hot if the shore polarity is reversed, which can present all kinds of problems involving both safety and electrolysis. You can buy a plug-in circuit tester that will immediately show, by means of three neon lights, whether the wiring is correct, has reversed polarity, open ground wire, open neutral wire, open hot wire, hot and ground reversed, or hot wire on neutral terminal with hot terminal unwired.

If you plug into strange marinas when off cruising, consider a circuit tester a necessity. Using a 120-volt test lamp, touch the black wire (hot) and the ground. The light should go on. When the white wire (neutral) and the ground are touched, it should not. A sonic alarm also can be permanently wired into the AC circuit. It gives a loud buzz if the polarity is reversed—usually audible 50 feet away.

That's all we'll say about AC.

Other ways exist to recharge your battery besides running the engine or plugging into shore power. But each of them involves considerable outlay of money, and probably you would not give any one of them the entire job of maintaining your batteries at the proper charge level. So we'll just take a quick look at each of them, and say something about what they might be able to do for you. For a more detailed discussion of each device, I recommend Daniel Spurr's *Upgrading The Cruising Sailboat,* and read Chapter 12—"Generating Electrical Power."

## SOLAR CELLS

A solar cell is a photovoltaic (light-versus-voltage) device. The most common ones now on the market are light-sensitive semiconducting silicon diodes. Silicon crystals are "doped" with very small amounts of carefully-controlled impurities to form a P-type region (positive) and an N-type region (negative). In a solar cell the P-type region is on top, where it is exposed to sunlight and the N-type region is the base. When light strikes the surface, electrons are driven across the junction between the two regions. The charge imbalance establishes a voltage that causes electrons to flow through an external circuit.

Each cell, however, produces only about half a volt, so a whole gang of them have to be connected in series to produce the 14 volts needed to recharge a battery. Most commercially-available marine solar panels contain 36 cells. The current in a series circuit is the same through each component, as we learned back in Chapter 2, so the entire panel current is determined by the surface area of any one cell. The conversion of solar energy to electrical energy is only 10 to 12% efficient with these devices.

According to solar cell data provided by Solar Power Corporation, 36 cells 9-centimeters in diameter wired in series gives 1.54 amps at the charging voltage of 14.4 volts under peak watt conditions. A peak watt is defined as the power delivered when incident power (sunlight) is 100 milliwatts per square centimeter. This converts to 0.156 amp (or 156 milliamps) per square inch of cell surface area or 0.024 amp per square centimeter of surface.

What this all boils down to is that solar cell panels still are too expensive for use on cruising boats owned by working stiffs like me. Some gold platers and highly specialized long-distance racing sailboats do find them useful regardless of cost. Some recent (1984) list prices for three different sized 36-cell units in teak frames are:

| | | |
|---|---|---|
| 10 watts, | 22" L × 11 ¾" W × 1" D, | $385. |
| 22 watts, | 22" L × 19 ¾" W × 1" D, | $616. |
| 44 watts, | 39 ¾" L × 19 ¾" W × 1" D, | $990. |

Figure 7–13: *Solar panel.*

You won't find these on old Miner's boat. I'd go back to kerosene before paying those prices. My advice is to use the sun to heat water and forget about making electricity with it—at least until the long-awaited price breakthrough for solar cells becomes a reality.

## WIND CHARGERS

Now wind chargers do make sense to me. Several of our cruising friends and liveaboards use them quite successfully. Just think how many times you have been on a mooring or at anchor when it was flat calm—not too many, I'll wager. Most wind chargers lend themselves to use at anchor and on moorings, where the vessel normally lies to the wind. That's only necessary with a fixed mounting, such as on the shrouds. You could use one in a slip, but you won't be very popular in a marina with a wind charger howling all night. Some howl (or whine) more than others, but I have yet to see what I would call a completely quiet one. Most noise appears to be from the propeller, rather than from the bearings or armature.

**Figure 7–14:** *Tom Colvin's* K'ung Fu Tse *with permanently mounted wind charger on wheelhouse.*

Wind chargers can be either permanently mounted so as to be used anytime, even while underway, or temporarily rigged for use while at anchor. Most cruisers will probably choose the temporary set-up; but then you have to be concerned about where the unit will live when not in use. Permanent installations, unless you live aboard a 48-foot junk like the Colvins' *K'ung Fu Tse*, will be restricted in size, including blade diameter, to that which can be accommodated aloft and out of the way (usually a mizzen mount) without causing too much windage. Whatever you hang up on that mast is surely going to work against you in a gale. Some permanent mast installations use the vertical axis Savonius rotor to minimize windage, but they provide such little output that they are not much more than toys —something like 300 milliamps (about ⅓ amp) at 40 knots of breeze, or 90 ma at a more reasonable 15 knots. Why bother? I would not consider buying a unit if it would not produce a couple of amps within the normal 12 to 20-knot windspeed range. Otherwise they're not much more than trickle chargers. Another way to evaluate wind chargers is to check what wind speed is necessary to start them. In general, the lower the better. There usually are more light air days than heavy ones; we just remember the gales better.

Aboard *Integrity* we have not yet succumbed to the lure of onboard refrigeration. But we are finding it more difficult to get good block ice when off cruising. Most everyone has cubes for sale, at exorbitant prices, but they don't last long. Over the past few years I have concluded that when it is time to refrigerate the ice box, I'll install a package electric compressor unit and wind charger at the same time. In case you're wondering, yes, I did look into kerosene and gas refrigerators. But I was horrfied by the fuel consumption figures quoted me for a CNG unit.

## WATER CHARGERS

Generations of sailors have dragged taffrail log spinners through the water behind them to record distance travelled, and more recently speed and distance. Then the device was electrified by attaching the spinner to a generator and reading output with a meter instead of the old "log clock." Use a bigger spinner to drive a bigger generator and you have a water charger.

The fluid coupling between water and propeller is much greater than between air and propeller, so you can expect much greater charging current at low speeds from a water charger device. But you'll pay for it in drag and, unfortunately, drag tends to increase with the square of speed—go twice as fast, you'll get four times as much drag. For most heavy-laden cruising boats, this is no big deal. If we were in a hurry we wouldn't be off cruising in the first place. Ocean-racing sailboats might have some qualms about introducing any drag at all. That's probably why they prefer using solar panels.

Water chargers come in two general configurations, one type is a towed propeller coupled to an on-deck generator, or an in-the-water prop-and-hub generator assembly. In the latter, the

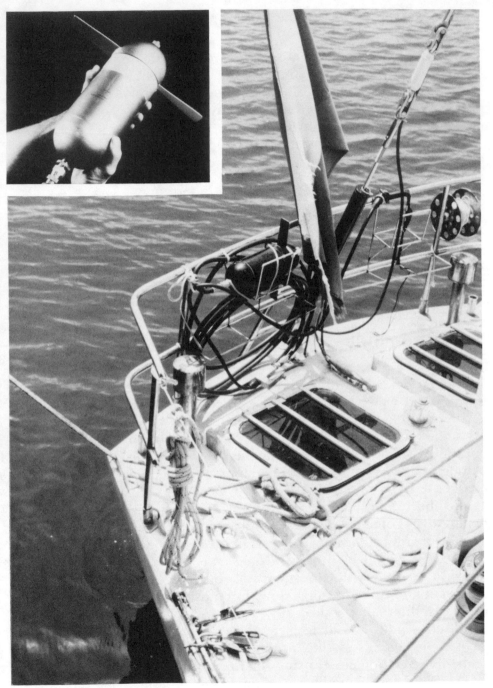

**Figure 7–15:** *Water charger.*

towing cable also is the power cable. Another type looks like an electric outboard motor that clamps onto the transom. That is essentially what it is, only it works backwards. Water turns the prop to generate charging current. I don't know anyone who has used one of these units, but their performance specifications look good—lots of charging amps at normal cruising speeds. Remember, however, that any energy output from the generator is at the expense of the net energy the sails have converted to the useful work of moving the boat.

If you are a tinkerer, you might want to check out a project in the *12 Volt Doctor's Handbook* that describes how to rewire an alternator to make your own wind or water charger.

## PORTABLE GASOLINE GENERATORS

I never really thought very much of these little portable AC/DC generators. In the first place, I never store any gasoline or other explosive fuel aboard. I'd rather row my dinghy several miles, or sail it, before hanging an outboard motor on its transom. Up until recently, I've considered portable generators as falling somewhere between a toy and a real device. I have been wrong before. My cruising acquaintances tell me they are reliable, durable, fairly quiet, safe and provide adequate output for their intended use. But the kicker came when I saw the photograph of Danny Greene in Dan Spurr's *Upgrading The Cruising Sailboat*, drilling a hole using his beat-up 7-year-old Honda that "still starts every time," despite the nicks, dents and rust. They must be good.

Perusing the catalogs for portable generators is like roaming through a motorcycle show. Familiar names are Honda, Kawasaki, Yamaha and Nissan. And the cases all look alike, too. The smallest practical size is 600 watts, but if you read the small print you'll see the cautionary note telling you to make sure your load requires less than 450 watts continuously. The 600 watt rating is for AC at 120 volts, the DC for battery charging is a little over 8 amps maximum, which makes it about 100 watts DC. These units come in various sizes, up to a couple of kilowatts (kw).

The next time I move aboard for an extended period of time with my computer, I'll probably use one of these generators to power it, as several of my cruising friends who are writers already do. I'm convinced. But by that time I'll bet we'll have book-sized portable computers that run on 12-volt DC or, better yet, that run off batteries charged by the sun!

## CHAPTER 8

# TROUBLESHOOTING THE SYSTEM

## TROUBLESHOOTING PRINCIPLES

Troubleshooting, as the name implies, refers to locating problems or faults, analyzing what is wrong, and then remedying the situation. Let's look at each of these procedures briefly to see what is involved in learning how to troubleshoot a boat's electrical system. So far we have covered the fundamental principles and basic theory we need to do it. We know about the wires, the sources, the controls and the transducers. We know what each separate item is and what it does in a circuit. But troubleshooting is an integrating experience—this is where it all has to come together. I'm reminded of my own training in aircraft engine mechanics at the Naval Air Technical Training Command at Memphis, Tennessee, nearly 30 years ago. Six months of schooling, classes and shop work, all came together during the final week on the flight line. The troubleshooting instructors were geniuses at screwing up an engine—some wouldn't start, some would start but not run, and others would run for a while and then quit. A crew's reward for fixing one problem would be to get a more challenging one next. But that was the best experience in the world. (We Marine Corps graduates of the school got to go back to Korea for a second trip. The flunk-outs got orders to Hawaii and Miami. Somehow I never quite saw the justice in that, but nobody said life was fair.)

To start with, how do you know when you have a fault or problem that needs fixing? There isn't a single answer to that question. Some are obvious, such as when you turn on a switch and nothing happens. Others are more subtle—a device comes on but quits after a while, or works only half-heartedly. And then there are the ones that really drive you crazy—intermittents—sometimes they work and other times they don't. They always work fine when you get the tools out to fix them, like the tooth that stops hurting on the way to the dentist. Something doesn't work properly. That's the first clue.

The next step, analysis, just means figuring out what is wrong. Weston Farmer, one of my favorite boating writers and designers, used to call this "noodling"; using your head plus experience plus some seat-of-the-pants instinct to determine what is causing the problem. If the battery is dead, where did the charge go? What drained it? If a circuit blows fuses, don't put any more in until you find out why they blow. Otherwise the next one will blow, too, and the only thing you'll learn is how expensive fuses are.

The key to becoming a good troubleshooter is developing a systematic approach. You can't just jump from one part of a system to another helter-skelter and expect your efforts to be successful.

Remedying a fault or problem is the easy part. Once you know what's wrong, it usually is fairly clear what you must do to repair it. Most often fixing will mean replacing a non-functioning item—screwing in a new bulb, replacing a fuse, or wiring a new device into the circuit.

## TROUBLESHOOTING INSTRUMENT: THE MULTIFUNCTION METER

Most troubleshooting can be done with few or no instruments. A meter is a handy device to have with you, but is not absolutely necessary for a lot of electrical detective work. A simple set of test lights can reveal a whole lot about how a circuit is working. If you are outfitting a set of electrical tools, I would recommend including a meter if you can afford one. But you don't have to spend $50 to $100 to get the best meter in the store. Just remember, as with all your tools, that this one will live aboard with you during the boating season. Its life will not be the same as if it sat on your home tool bench, nice and dry. For 10 years now I have carried one of Radio Shack's least expensive models, which I built from a kit. I think it cost $7.95 then. A similar meter, all wired, costs only $10.95 today. I have to keep a rubber band around mine to hold it together, but it still works. Maybe next year I'll get a new one.

These meters illustrated here carry list prices of from $10.95 to $34.95 in the 1984 catalog, but usually one of the meters is on sale at any time, so check your local papers for specials and save some money. Any of them is perfectly adequate for our purposes. The folding meter, new this year, folds shut and latches, protecting it from banging around in a boat locker.

Test meters are called multimeters or multitesters, which means that one meter can be used to measure several different electrical units rather than having to buy separate meters to read volts, amps and ohms. Sometimes they are called VOM for Volt—Ohm—Meter. The smallest meter will have up to 8 different ranges, including several ranges of AC and DC volts, one or more ohm ranges, and one or more ranges of DC milliamps. Some larger meters will read up to 10 amps DC. So one meter is capable of making measurements of voltage, current and resistance—everything we need to analyze a circuit. Bigger and more expensive meters generally have many more ranges and/ or other features, such as a "beep" continuity tester. Newer models use LCD digital display for meter readings, which is nice on a test bench, but doesn't help much for troubleshooting on your boat.

All multimeters include at least one dry cell inside. You can't read ohms without it. All the meters shown use one AA cell. Some larger meters use a 9-volt battery as well. These cells last a long time, so it is easy to forget all about them. Make it a point to check the cell at the beginning of each boating season. If it looks corroded or is not functioning properly, replace it. Don't risk ruining a good meter for a 27-cent dry cell. Use more expensive "alkaline" cells, which last a very long time and usually don't leak. There are plenty of other good test meters on

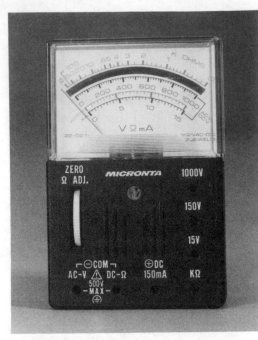

**Figure 8–1:** *The 8-range pocket sized multitester is an inexpensive, adequate troubleshooting meter. (Courtesy of Radio Shack.)*

**Figure 8–2:** *The 18-range multitester for home, shop or boat costs more, does a little more. (Courtesy of Radio Shack.)*

**Figure 8–3:** *25-range folding multitester looks rugged for a delicate meter. (Courtesy of Radio Shack.)*

**Figure 8–4:** *The 27-range multitester has more features than you will normally need for most troubleshooting. (Courtesy of Radio Shack.)*

the market besides the ones illustrated. I chose to show Radio Shack models because their products have always given me good service for the price and because the stores are everywhere.

Wherever you get your meter, read the instruction booklet carefully before attempting to use it. The meter will come with 2 loose test leads, a black one and a red one. On inexpensive meters the various functions and ranges are selected by where the leads are plugged into the meter. It seems confusing at first, but follow the manufacturer's specific instructions. More expensive meters use a rotary switch to select ranges and functions, but still have several places to plug in the leads. The red lead is always used to connect the meter to the positive side of the circuit. The black lead always goes to negative. The black lead plugs into one of the common "(−) COM" sockets on the meter. The red lead plugs into the desired function or range, if no switch is used, or else into the plug marked "(+) V − Ω − A." In some cases, as in measuring resistance, it doesn't make any difference which way the leads connect to the piece to be tested. But always make it a point to hook up the meter leads properly.

### READING OHMS

Let's see how to measure resistance. First plug in the leads. If there is only one ohm scale the plug will be marked KΩ. If more than one ohm scale, the switch will indicate R × 1 (read the ohm scale directly), R × 10 (multiply the numbers by 10), R × 1K (multiply the numbers by 1000), etc. The ohm scale usually is the top one and it will have zero on the right end, backwards from all the other scales. The left end will read infinity (a sideways eight), which just means too high to read. All meters will have an OHMS ADJUST or ZERO switch. Touch the test lead tips together and read the scale. The needle should jump over to the low end when the tips touch. Turn the adjust switch until the meter reads zero. Try a couple of times to make sure the needle always comes back to zero. Now the meter is ready to measure some unknown resistance. If you can't zero the meter you need a new dry cell. Ohmmeters measure resistance by responding to a small current, which flows from their internal dry cell through a known internal resistor plus the unknown external resistance. That's why the circuit must always be turned off or disconnected while making a resistance measurement. When the leads are touched together, there is no external resistance, so a maximum current flows and the needle swings to the high end of the scale—which is marked zero ohms, no external resistance. The more the external resistance, the lower the meter current, and the less deflection of the needle, so you read higher ohm values down toward the left end of the scale. A precaution: when measuring resistance, make sure that firm contact is being made, otherwise the resistance of the contact area itself may spoil the reading, especially in the lower ranges.

### READING DC VOLTS

To read volts DC, plug the black lead into the proper common socket, the red lead into the "15 V" or "(+) V−Ω−A" socket and then dial a range larger than you expect to read. For your boat, dial the next number higher than 12, which could be 15, 25 or 30, depending on the meter used. If you read only a few volts, you can always come down to a lower range after you determine it is safe to do so. You generally get a better reading on the lowest safe scale. If you start too low, you may damage the meter or blow its fuse. Voltage readings always are made while the circuit is "hot" or energized. The meter always is connected "across" or in parallel with the item whose voltage you want to know. This means that it is very easy to get voltage measurements—just touch the test lead tips to any two exposed points in the circuit and read the proper volts scale. But the red lead always has to touch the positive end of the circuit, and the black lead the negative. Reverse polarity and the needle tries to go the other way. Also, each scale reads differently. Before you can interpolate between numbers, you first must determine how much each small scale subdivision represents. You will get used to it in time, but it is something you have to think about each time you make a reading. Internally, the voltmeter circuit contains a high resistance, which allows only a small portion of the main circuit current to flow through the meter to cause the needle to deflect.

## READING AC VOLTS

If you have a shore power connector to a battery charger, or use an inverter or a gasoline AC generator, you may need to measure AC volts sometime. Plug the black lead into the AC-V socket and the red into the 150V socket. The test leads can be touched into a connector plug or to exposed contacts. Just make sure you hold the leads with the insulated handles, and not with any part of the metal tips. Even if you reverse the red and black test lead tips to the connector plug you will still read close to 120 volts, either way. But between black and green ground you'll also read 120 volts; between white and green, zero. The latter is the test for proper polarity which we mentioned earlier back in Chapter 7.

## READING DC AMPS

Actually, most test meters will measure only DC milliamps; but if your meter does read amps, the testing is done the same way. This function is used much less than the others because the circuit must be physically disconnected and the meter inserted into the main circuit in series in order to get a measurement. The ammeter part of the test meter has an extremely low resistance; all of the circuit current has to pass through it without causing power loss, or the readings it gives will be incorrect. One place the ammeter function can be used is to locate electrical leaks at the battery. I'll tell you about that later.

To make a milliamp reading, open the circuit by disconnecting a wire end at some convenient point and separating the parts. Touch the red test lead tip to the positive end and the black test lead to the negative end. This puts the meter into the circuit and shows how much current is present in that whole portion of the circuit. Remember to reconnect the wire after making the reading. Measuring AC current is best done with a snap-on AC ammeter, which does not require breaking the circuit. It just snaps around the wire carrying a current and gives a reading.

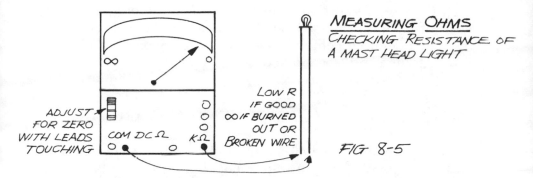

**MEASURING OHMS**
CHECKING RESISTANCE OF
A MAST HEAD LIGHT

LOW R
IF GOOD
∞ IF BURNED
OUT OR
BROKEN WIRE

ADJUST
FOR ZERO
WITH LEADS
TOUCHING

COM DC Ω    KΩ

FIG 8-5

**Figure: 8–5:** *Checking resistance of a masthead light.*

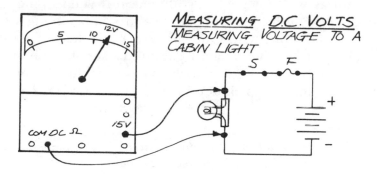

**MEASURING D.C. VOLTS**
MEASURING VOLTAGE TO A
CABIN LIGHT

S    F

+

15V

COM DC Ω

−

**Figure 8–6:** *Measuring voltage to a cabin light.*

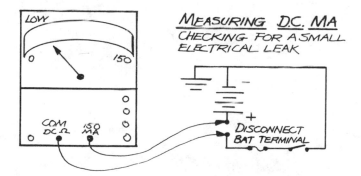

**MEASURING D.C. MA**
CHECKING FOR A SMALL
ELECTRICAL LEAK

LOW

0    150

COM
DC Ω    150
MA

DISCONNECT
BAT TERMINAL

+

**Figure 8–7:** *Checking for a small electrical leak.*

I will close this section on using your multimeter with a final word of caution: always check the function and range setting of the meter before touching the test leads to any part of a circuit. It only takes a split second to destroy a meter.

## TROUBLESHOOTING INSTRUMENT: TEST LIGHTS

As I said before, a whole lot of troubleshooting can be done with a couple of test lights. Store-bought models can be found in most auto supply or parts stores for a couple of dollars, but you can cobble up a home-brewed set out of a junk box. It will work just as well for next to nothing. So if you're pinched for money while outfitting your electrical troubleshooting kit, pass on the meter for a while, maybe Santa will leave one under your bowsprit next Christmas. But build a set of test lights.

There are two test lights that we will look at first: a continuity light and a test lamp. Later I'll tell you about an LED leak tester and how to make an inexpensive one.

**Figure 8–8:** *Manufactured equipment on left, homemade on right. Continuity tester at top, 12-volt test light below.*

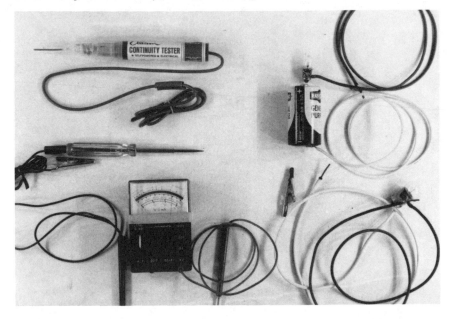

## A CONTINUITY TESTER

First the continuity tester. I found the manufactured model in a local home and auto store selling for $1.99, which includes the bulb but not the two AA dry cells that fit inside the plastic body. It is, essentially, a flashlight without a switch to turn it on. It must be used only on portions of circuits that are turned off, since it works on its own 3 volts. Twelve volts from the main circuit would blow the bulb. Continuity means continuous or complete. A complete circuit has continuity, an incomplete one does not. You test for continuity by touching both leads of the tester to some part of a circuit. If it is continuous or unbroken the bulb will light. No continuity, no light. Test to make sure it is working by touching the ends together—the bulb should light.

## MAKE YOUR OWN

If you have a spare C or D cell and a flashlight bulb and a couple pieces of wire on hand, you can make your own for nothing which will work just as well. Even if you have to buy the cell and bulb, you'll come out way ahead. Solder one piece of wire to the side of the bulb base (not the tip). Solder the other wire to the bottom of the cell. That's all there is to it. You or your mate will have to hold the bulb on to the cell center terminal while you are using it to make tests, but that's no big deal. You will soon learn to hold them together in the palm of one hand while you work the other ends of the wires with the other hand. Not very elegant, I'll admit. But it's inexpensive and it works. My kind of tester.

## BUYING OR MAKING TEST LIGHTS

The test light is even simpler. Find a single-filament 12-volt auto lamp. One will cost about 50 cents if you have to buy it. Find two more pieces of wire and solder one to the tip of the base and the other to the side. This tester has to be used on a "hot" or energized circuit. If there is voltage to where you touch the ends, it will light. The brightness of the light will tell you something about how much current is passing through the bulb, the brighter the light the more the current. I found an "Auto Tester" in the same home and auto store also selling for $1.99. It looks something like a screwdriver with a wire and aligator clip coming out of the top. The tip end is pointed and there is a light in the plastic handle that comes on when the ends make contact with 6 or 12 volts. This one also can be used for timing ignition on foreign cars.

## LOCATING FAULTS

Let's start with some easy problems.

### LIGHT WON'T WORK

The sun has set, twilight is fading into darkness. You reach for the light switch, flip it and nothing happens. You've got a problem. If you are at anchor, and it is a cabin light, it's not such a big deal—maybe some other light will work, or you can light a kerosene lamp or a candle. But if you are underway crossing a shipping lane and it's your navigation lights that don't come on, then it is a big deal, not only for you and your vessel and your crew's safety and survival, but now you are violating the rules of the road and could be penalized. In both cases, you recognize you have a problem. Finding a solution is more imperative in the second.

### MOISTURE-RELATED PROBLEMS

How about a cabin light or a navigation side light that will not work when it rains, but works fine when it is dry? That's a harder problem. We seldom feel like working on things when it is raining, but it sounds like that may be the only time to find out what is causing the problem. The worst thing about this problem is you probably won't like what you find as the culprit. The problem with the light is electrical, but it may well be that the cause of the problem is a leaky wooden deck or a leaking fiberglass hull-to-deck joint. Now the complete solution to the problem is much more extensive (and expensive).

### ENGINE WON'T START

You've spent the night in Onset Harbor so you can get underway first thing in the morning and catch the changing fair tide through the Cape Cod Canal at 0615—a good start on your first cruise "Downeast." You rouse your crew at first light, have a quick breakfast, and get ready to break out the anchor. You hit your diesel starter switch—and nothing happens. Stone cold dead. No doubt about it, that's a problem. As distressing as these sound, they are the easy problems.

### BILGE PUMP PROBLEM

You are heading for Key West via the Inside Passage through Florida Bay in your retired wooden lobster boat converted to family cruiser. She's old and slow, but faithful and so comfortable. The bilge pump cycles about every 30 minutes or so, and spits back what looks like half a bucket of seawater. Next cycle the stream flows, then stops, but you hear the whine of the pump continuing above the muffled rumble of the engine. The slap of a wave against the hull may make it stop, but you've got a problem—one that likely will get worse and maybe cause considerable grief in the future.

### BLINKING MASTHEAD LIGHT

Now you are cruising Chesapeake Bay in your 10-year-old 32-foot fiberglass cruising sailboat. That's not very old as far as the boat is concerned, but old enough for lots of different kinds of electrical problems to develop. The wind has died so you are powering into Annapolis. You notice your masthead (or steaming) light is blinking—erratically, not in code, but it is surely telling you something. It may be a loose bulb, a loose connection in the socket—or anywhere in the circuit, a chafed wire shorting to the mast, or any of several other possibilities. This one may be difficult to find.

We'll work through these common examples to show you how to approach solving all boat electrical problems.

## NOODLING OUT A SOLUTION

When you are confronted by any electrical problem, you have to be prepared to attack it systematically and logically. An old-timer acquaintance of mine was fond of saying, "Electrical problems are easy—it's either a short or a break." That's rather oversimplified, but basically he was correct. Finding and fixing the shorts and breaks is something else again, though. If your boat came with an owner's manual (most don't), and if it happened to contain a complete wiring diagram for the whole boat (most don't), then you are in tall clover when it comes to noodling out a solution to an electrical problem.

A wiring diagram is your blueprint to success in troubleshooting—as long as you can read one and follow your way around the various circuits. Back in Chapter 2, when we described the various circuit elements and showed how they went together, we were laying the groundwork for you to analyze and solve your own electrical problems.

### MAKE A PICTURE

What if you don't have a factory wiring diagram? Make your own, of course. If you don't like the standard symbols we showed you, don't use them; devise your own. If you can't find a symbol for bilge pump, make a little box and put B.P. in it and show two dots for hook-up points. The whole purpose in making a sketch is you will see what parts are in the circuit, and how they are hooked together. Once you make this drawing you will have a map for analyzing the problem.

Now let's look at one of those problems we were talking about, the old wooden cruiser on its way to Key West whose bilge pump kept running. The problem sounds fairly straightforward, most likely a hanging-up float switch, usually caused by bilge crud, lint, dog hair, etc. Most electric bilge pump installations use a 3-position (ON-OFF-AUTOMATIC) switch either in addition to the control panel switch or in place of it, and a float switch for automatic operation, which may be built into the pump housing. Here's how to make a simple sketch of that system, without using many standard symbols.

That wasn't so hard was it? The sketch doesn't have to be fancy or pretty in order to be useful. It does show us that while the float switch could be the culprit while in Automatic, it is not the only possible cause of trouble. If the wires chafe through the insulation, the float switch "hot" wire could short to the ON wire, bypass the float switch, and cause the same result. You might not think about these alternatives unless you had a picture to look at. That is the real value of making a

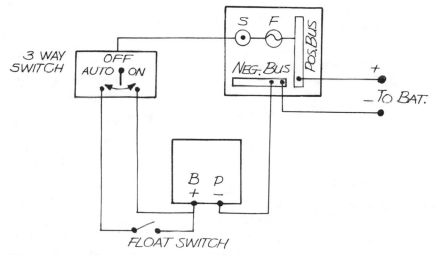

**Figure 8–9:** *If you don't remember the standard bilge pump circuit symbols, make up your own, but make the sketch. It will help you.*

sketch, to focus your attention on all the possibilities, not just the obvious ones. It is discouraging when you buy a new float switch, install it, and the problem persists. You have to make sure the unit is defective before you replace it. A lot of would-be troubleshooters waste their money needlessly by not analyzing the situation completely before jumping in and making repairs harum-scarum.

Let's follow through on this problem. The pump works when it is supposed to, it just doesn't stop working. The control panel fuse and switch or circuit breaker would not cause that problem, nor would anything upstream of them. The fault is probably between the 3-position switch and the pump. Turn off the circuit at the panel or remove the fuse. Examine the switch as much as possible, looking for corrosion or signs of arcing (usually discoloration). Use your continuity test lamp to see whether you get continuity from center terminal to either end when the switch is thrown, and break in continuity when it is turned off. If you are checking with your multimeter, the ohms scale should read zero for continuity and infinity for off. If the switch checks OK, follow the wires along their entire length to the bilge. Feel the wires; you're looking for signs of damage to the insulation, chafing, cracks and loose or corroded terminal connectors. It will be easier to lift up the float switch and bilge pump to the cabin sole for examination, but put them on some rags or old newspapers to protect the sole. Bilge goop is dreadful stuff.

If the float switch is a separate unit, look at it first, especially around the hinge. Any crud or corrosion built up on it? Lift the float up gently. If it's a mechanical, rather than a mercury switch, can you hear it turn on? Let it go down—hear it click off? Test it for continuity between the switch terminals. The light should go on when the switch is up (zero ohms), off when it's down (infinity ohms). Do this gently, you are simulating the slowly falling bilge water level. If the switch is built into the pump, you may have more trouble getting meter or continuity light tests. Put your ear to the pump and work the switch. Can you hear anything happening? Perform the meter or light tests if you can. If you can't, energize the circuit at the panel (switch or fuse), set the pump and float switch upright, put the 3-position switch to automatic, and gently lift the float until the pump starts working. Then let it down gently and see whether the pump cuts out at the bottom position. If it does not, you need to buy a new float switch—or attempt to repair this one. Don't let the pump run too long without water. If everything works OK now, as it sometimes does, you might as well put it back and wait for the problem to reappear. But before you do that, and as long as you are this dirty, go ahead and clean the bilge thoroughly. Use a rag, not paper towels or sponge; they only leave more debris. Get up all loose lint, sawdust, hairs, and other particles you can find. Chances are that whatever was causing the problem dislodged itself when you lifted up the float switch and pump. Make sure that it doesn't come back too soon.

## FOLLOW A SYSTEM

How about the engine that wouldn't start on the west end of the Cape Cod Canal? It sounds like a dead battery to me, too. But it doesn't have to be. It could be anything in the starter circuit causing the problem. Make another sketch showing all the items you can think of in the starter circuit. Numbers refer to the tests we will make with our troubleshooting light.

Let's see, from battery to battery master or selector switch (in

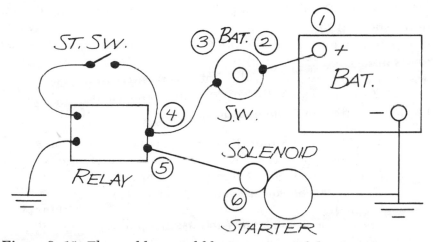

**Figure 8–10:** *The problem could be in any one of the starter circuit components. Check it out systematically.*

one's haste to get underway, it's possible to forget to turn this on), then to the starter relay with a side branch through the engine control panel and starter switch (key or push button), which allows us to use small wires for low current to the switch. When the switch is closed the relay closes and carries heavy current to the solenoid and starter. The relay and solenoid may be combined, or separate, it depends on your engine and starter assembly. The problem could be in any of these items or in the connecting wires between them. We can check this out with our 12-volt test lamp or by using a meter set to the 15-volt DC scale. There is a tendency to want to begin at the starter, since it was the thing we found not working. But you will save time in the long run if you learn *always begin where the electric current starts, the battery.* That way we will check everything in order and determine that we have voltage and current to that point. As soon as we don't have it, we have located the fault.

**Figure 8–11:** *Large and small alligator clips.*

Take your 12-volt test lamp, homemade or store bought, and hook one end to the engine block common ground (an alligator clip is handy for this; Radio Shack sells many sizes for about 20 cents apiece—get an assortment). Use the other end as a probe and work your way from the battery positive terminal to the starter, but first check the ground strap between the negative battery terminal and the engine to make sure it is tight.

1. Touch the (+) terminal, bright light shows good charge; dim or no light, very low battery. In the latter case, you know you need a recharge before you can crank the engine, or maybe you can start it by hand. If you get a good bright light on (+), check the terminals for condition. Loosen the terminal nuts and use the puller to lift off the terminal connectors. Clean them shiny bright and reinstall, tighten nuts.
2. Move the test probe to the battery or selector switch, battery side first. Bright light here says the battery connector is good.
3. Go to the ON side (or 1 or 2 or Both) and test. Bright light here says the main switch is good, no light says it is not turned on, or it's bad and needs replacing.
4. Go to the battery side of the relay. Bright light here says the wiring to it is OK.
5. Go to the other (starter) side of the relay with the probe and hit the starter switch. Bright light now shows that BOTH the starter switch and relay are functioning properly. No light could be caused by either one not working. Check the starter switch by turning the key or pushing the starter button and wiggling the switch. If the light flickers the switch is bad. Inside the relay there could be two problems, either the coil is open and not working when the starter switch is closed, or the heavy duty points are burned and could be stuck. With the switch open, you should read continuity with some resistance between the switch side terminals of the relay—if not, the coil is no good, replace the Relay.
6. Touch the battery terminal on the solenoid and turn on the starter switch. A bright light here means that the trouble has to be with the starter or solenoid. Before you pull them off, check to see if the starter is loose on the engine. The starter has to complete its circuit back to the negative battery terminal through the engine block. If its retaining

bolts have been loosened by vibration, the connection may be broken. Tightening may be all you need to make it work; otherwise, with good voltage to the starter the fault must lie in the solenoid or the starter motor. They come off together and will have to be taken to a shop for checkout.

## TICKLING THE FIELD

If you left some light or a TV on all night and your batteries are down completely, even if you get the diesel engine started by hand cranking, the alternator may not recharge them. That's because alternators require some current in the field to make them work. Generators always had some residual magnetism in the field poles to get them started charging; this is not true for alternators. But don't despair, there is a way out by "tickling" the field with a small current from some dry cells.

If you happen to have a lantern battery aboard, you're in good shape. One of those should be enough to get things started. Otherwise, gather up all the flashlight or penlight cells you can find in your portable radios, etc. and line them up in series, head to tail. Use tape or rubber bands to hold them together. Run one wire from the top end center terminal ( + ) and another wire from the last base ( − ). Touch the ( + ) wire to the field connector on the regulator and the ( − ) wire to the alternator case while you squeeze the line of cells together. Once the alternator pumps some life into the battery, it will take over the operation and you can remove the dry cells from the circuit.

## SIMPLE PROBLEMS WITH VARYING DEGREES OF COMPLEXITY

I'm going to bring this analysis section to a close by looking at several problems involving lights—one simple, the others more complex. Let's do a cabin light first. In most cases this problem is solved by common sense, which you didn't need this book for. You turn on the switch on the chart light over the navigation station and nothing happens. I wouldn't draw a wiring diagram just yet. Like most people, I would remove the cover (if the lamp had one), unscrew the bulb and examine it. Can you see if the filament is broken? Try shaking the bulb to see if you can hear pieces rattling around. If it is frosted so you can't see inside, give it a continuity test between the center tip and side. If the bulb flunks any of these tests, replace it. Most of the time that will solve the problem. Not much analysis needed here.

Now let's go one step further. The light in the head doesn't work. Neither does the one on that side of the forward cabin, nor the one over the settee—all the starboard cabin lights are out. Port side lights are all OK. Now this is a problem that'll require troubleshooting. All those bulbs didn't burn out at the same time. This is a circuit problem. The starboard cabin lights are all connected in parallel to the same interior circuit with a circuit breaker or switch and fuse in the control panel. Instead of looking at all the bulbs, now we should go to the control panel. Is the switch turned off? Maybe someone hit it by mistake. Is the breaker tripped? Wonder why? Pull the fuse out and examine it. Is it blown? If the switch was off, turn it on. But if the breaker was tripped or the fuse blown, check a little further before resetting or putting in a new fuse. If there was a reason for the overload, you've got to find it or else the same thing will happen again. Perhaps one of the lights was added without recalculating the total circuit load, which we discussed in the section on parallel circuits in Chapter 2. You may never know there is a problem until all the lights are turned on at once—then the fuse blows or the breaker trips. Now maybe a circuit diagram will help. Make it simple, but as complete as possible. Like this:

**Figure 8–12:** *A fault in one branch of the starboard cabin lights parallel circuit will affect only that one item. If all are out, the fault must be upstream of the first branch point. Check the control panel switch first, then the fuse or breaker.*

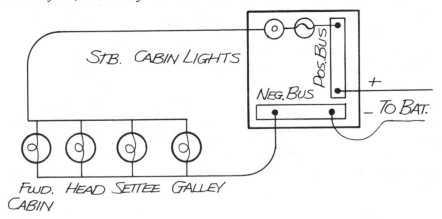

Here's where we get to use the arithmetic and magic triangles from the first two chapters in a practical situation. Follow along with me, and review those sections if necessary. Someday you may have to do the figuring on your own. First thing we had better do is check the wattage of each bulb and add them all up. Then divide the total power or sum of the wattage by 12 volts to get the current through the fuse and switch ($I = P/V$). Regular 12-volt cabin lamp bulbs can run from less than 15 watts up to 50 watts each. Let's assume our four bulbs are 25, 25, 25 and 50 watts; sum is 125 watts. Current is 125 watts/ 12 volts = 10.42 amps. No wonder the 10-amp fuse blew or the 10-amp breaker tripped when they all were turned on together.

How come we never had this trouble before? Oh yeah, remember how last year when the mate complained she couldn't see to do dishes in the galley, you went to the marina store and got a brighter bulb? Never really thought how that would affect things, did you? Most people don't. We're too used to thinking about our house circuits, where we can screw in just about any size bulb without causing problems. In this case, when all 4 bulbs used 25 watts each, the total power consumption was 100 watts, and the current through the panel was 8.33 amps; perfectly safe for the 10-amp fuse or breaker, even when they were all on at the same time. But when you changed the galley bulb to 50 watts, the whole circuit was affected. Not only did the current through that outlet double from 2.1 amps to 4.2 amps, but the total circuit resistance dropped from 1.44 ohms to 1.15 ohms—doesn't sound like much, but that is a 20% decrease. That's why the current went from a tolerable 8.33 amps to a fuse-blowing 10.4 amps.

How do you solve this one? The first impulse might be to put in a larger fuse, but that's NOT the way to solve this problem. The fuse is there to protect the circuit and the circuit is now overloaded. So some of the load must be removed. Remembering not to turn on all the lights together is the least expensive answer, but not always practical—especially if you have teenagers aboard. Replace the galley bulb with the original 25 watt one? The mate may then stop washing dishes—that's what got you into this problem in the first place. Maybe it is time to think about replacing one or more of the incandescent lights with more efficient fluorescent lamps. You can generally reduce your wattage by about half for the same light output. But remember, they can cause radio frequency interference, so don't go all fluorescent.

   Now let's consider one more light problem before we quit, so we can think about nitty-gritty stuff instead of theory. How about a sailboat with a non-functioning light up the mast somewhere (masthead, masttop tricolor or anchor)? It is one thing to have a burned-out cabin light; we solved that one by common sense. A non-functioning mast light may be the same problem, burned-out bulb, but it is made more difficult because of its location. And more things could be wrong besides the bulb. If the problem is up the mast, someone will have to go there to fix it; but before I climb a mast, I like to know that I really have to.

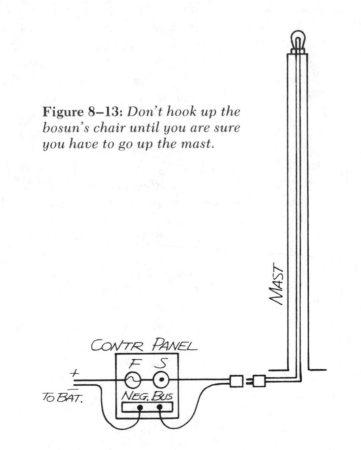

**Figure 8–13:** *Don't hook up the bosun's chair until you are sure you have to go up the mast.*

In this case, I would do things a little differently, because the mast wiring presents some special problems. You can make a diagram, as I have done, but it isn't as helpful here as in other situations, because each mast light is its own simple series circuit with its own switch. I first would look at the fuse or circuit breaker. If the fuse is blown or the breaker tripped, it indicates a more serious problem than a burned out bulb. If the fuse and breaker are OK, and other lights are working, then it is not a battery or master switch fault. Open up the control panel, and clip one lead from the 12-volt test lamp to the negative bus. First check the battery side of this fuse holder for a bright light, then the far side of fuse holder, next the battery side of switch, and then the far side of switch, watching the light come on when switch is closed. A bright light at each test point verifies the panel is OK. If so, close it up.

Next I would move to the base of the mast. What we have to find here is the connector plug or terminal strip disconnecting all the wires that run up the mast when the mast is pulled. This connector should be accessible for troubleshooting, but I have seen many factory-designed deck-mounted masts in which the connector is stuffed inside the mast before it drops on to the mast step. If mine were like that I'd change it, just for convenience during troubleshooting. Separate the connector into the mast end and boat end parts. Take your test lamp and stick the wires into the boat end part. It should light when the switch is closed. If so, you have power to the mast. Your problems are up in the air somewhere. You might as well have someone start looking for the bosun's chair.

Meanwhile, put away the test lamp and get out your continuity tester. Touch the two wires to the mast end of the connector. Continuity means the bulb and socket are good. If we're lucky here, we'll get no continuity, meaning the bulb is burned out. One other test to make here, especially if we had a blown fuse or tripped breaker, is to check continuity between each wire and the aluminum mast, one at a time. Continuity from either wire indicates a dead short to the grounded mast. That means a rewiring job, but not necessarily pulling the mast. You might be able to use the old wire to pull the new one into place as you remove the old one from the top. Nobody said this was easy, but if it works it will be quicker and less expensive than pulling the mast. You probably have noticed I like inexpensive best of all.

## LEAKS AND THEIR DETECTION

So the last thing we'll discuss, appropriately enough, is an inexpensive leak finder. These are electrical leaks we're talking about now, not water ones, although they often are interconnected. An electrical leak occurs whenever current finds some unwanted way to get from one place to another. Wires start out with good insulation to prevent or inhibit leakage. But in time the hostile salt air environment, the constant motion, and extremes of temperature take their toll. The insulation eventually chafes thinner, cracks and may be penetrated by moisture and salt air. Conducting paths other than the wire itself may develop between the circuit and ground, back to the negative terminal of the battery.

Electrical leaks pose two main problems on your boat:

1.  They constantly drain charge from the battery. You may notice this if you use the boat only on weekends. When you first come aboard, the battery voltage will be less than the full charge value. If the leak is bad enough, you might not be able to start the engine. This will get your attention every time, but by then it might be too late to prevent damage to your boat.
2.  Electrical leaks are an open invitation to metallic stray-current corrosion. Such currents can be quite damaging to the boat's hull (if metal) or its equipment in time, even though the current drain might appear to be negligible.

How do you find whether you have a leak or not? Here are three different methods, starting with the easiest. Get the 12-volt test lamp. Go to the battery and lift off the positive terminal connector. Make sure that all circuit switches are off (open), fuses in place, and the master battery switch is on. No current should be flowing in any circuit. Touch the test lamp leads between the positive post and the connector. There should be no light with no current. If you get a bright light, you have a big leak that you didn't know about—probably a switch inadvertently left closed, or one hanging up in the closed position, or a dead short in one of the circuits. Flip all the switches one at a time to see if it goes away. If not, pull the fuses out one at a time until the light is extinguished. The last one is your offending circuit. You had better fix this fault at once, because it is a serious drain on your battery, and because current straying into the water may be establishing a metal-eating electrolysis problem.

If you get a very dim glow of the test lamp, the more likely case, you still have a leak that can be serious, but it will drain your batteries much more slowly than the bright one will. A suspected faint dim glow warrants further inspection with your test meter. Set it for 15 volts DC and touch the red lead to the (+) battery terminal, black lead to the connector. If there is ANY leak, no matter how small, the meter will read 12 volts. If you want to see how much current is leaking, switch to the highest DC amps scale and see if you can read it. If not, keep reducing down the milliamp scales until you can get the reading. If you got 12 volts before, there is a leak, but it might be extremely small. If you don't get a current reading, switch the meter to ohms and adjust the zero. Now touch the leads this way: red to the loose connector and black to the negative battery post. Now you're trying to read the resistance of the leak circuit between the battery connector and ground—most likely a fairly high value. If it is less than 1000 ohms it must be found and fixed. Over 1000 ohms may be difficult to find, and will cause negligible current loss. Remember Ohm's Law? For 1000 ohms, the current will be 12 volts/1000 ohms = .012 amp or 12 ma. For 10,000 ohms forget it. That's just a consequence of living in a damp salt air environment.

The third method will cost you less than a buck. Make two testers from parts sold by Radio Shack stores. The things are so cheap that they come 2 in a pack, so make two and have a spare, or give one to a fellow boatowner. I poked around a Radio Shack store looking for something that would give a very sensitive leak test, and still be rugged, so as to not burn out easily if there were a short or high leakage present. A light emitting diode (LED) looked just right. The specs. on the package give "Forward Voltage 2.1 volts at 20 ma, Maximum current 30 ma." Now I needed a resistor to limit the current down to the operating range of 20 to 30 ma. A quick Ohm's Law calculation gave this:

$$R \text{ needed} = (V \text{ bat} - V \text{ fwd}) / I \text{ fwd}$$
$$R \text{ needed} = (13 \text{ volts} - 2.1 \text{ volts}) / .020 \text{ amp}$$
$$R \text{ needed} = 545 \text{ ohms}$$

In the resistor display I found some 560 ohm, ½-watt packages. Should be close enough. I bought 2 jumbo red LEDs for 69 cents and 2 of the 560 ohm resistors for 19 cents. I took these to my laboratory and ran a bunch of tests on them and experimented with some other resistors, too. This series combination worked just as expected. On dead short at 15 volts the current was a safe 23 milliamps without the resistor getting too hot. The LED indicator is so sensitive that it will blink on with currents as low as 1 milliamp at 1 volt. The parts are too small to photograph very well, so I'll just make a sketch for you of the LED leak finder. The LEDs come with two wire leads of unequal length; the longer is the positive (+) end. I soldered the resistor to the (+) end of the LED (you have to do it quickly), and then added a couple pieces of red and black wire as shown. You could fancy one up with a little plastic parts box and a couple of plug-in test leads if you wanted to, but it won't work any better.

To use this homemade leak detector, follow the same procedure as outlined in the test lamp method. This detector will give a positive indication, even for the smallest of leaks. Make sure the detector is placed between the positive post and the connector and that you connect the positive end to the positive battery post and the negative end to the connector.

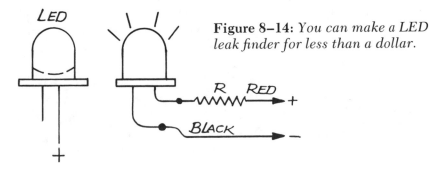

**Figure 8–14:** *You can make a LED leak finder for less than a dollar.*

Troubleshooting is the challenging and fun part of doing your own electrical work. The feeling of satisfaction you get when you find something wrong, figure out what it is, and then fix it is especially rewarding. So is the money you save by being able to do it. The two most important lessons about troubleshooting that I can give you are these:

1. Be systematic and logical in your analysis.
2. Always think before you act.

# EPILOG

If you understood electric theory as we went along, followed the various examples and calculations we occasionally had to make, learned to work systematically and to think analytically in searching for a solution to a problem, and have some idea of the tools and testers needed and how to use them, then you are ready to go off on your own. There is not much else anyone can do for you. You just need to gain experience, and that's entirely up to you. Now don't immediately jump in and start rewiring your boat if it is working OK now. Remember the old-timer's injunction: "If it ain't broke, don't fix it!." But you are ready to begin a regular program of systematic preventive maintenance, which many people ignore until it is too late. The whole idea here is to prevent problems by finding discrepancies early enough, and correcting them so they don't grow into problems. Also, your curiosity should be piqued enough to make you want to learn more about what makes electrical things work. Many units are sealed to protect them from the hostile environment. Don't try to open these. Instead, you might find one that has been replaced because it didn't work. The boatyard or marina electrician may have some old junk parts that he will let you have, but don't expect him to teach you his trade so you can do your own work and not hire him.

Where do we begin a preventive maintenance program? I'd start with the battery or batteries. At least once a week, daily if you are doing a lot of powering, check the electrolyte level in each cell, not just the one that's easiest to get at. Remember that each cell is separate from the others, so each must be looked at. One of the first signs of battery trouble is indicated by excessive water consumption. So pay attention if one cell seems to need water more often than the others, it's trying to tell you something. Get a battery hydrometer and occasionally check the specific gravity of each cell—once a month should be OK unless you are experiencing some other problems like water consumption or habitually low battery charge. Keep the battery clean. Some of those leaks we talked about might be caused by conducting paths of crud. Some left over dish water will work fine for cleaning the battery top. If you should spill some of the electrolyte from the hydrometer, wipe it up with a neutralizing solution of baking soda in water. Keep the battery terminals shiny clean.

Every 4 to 6 weeks pull the connectors off with the terminal puller tool and check. If they are not shiny inside, and the posts shiny on the outside, clean them with the proper tools, or a knife blade or some sandpaper but get them clean. Then replace and tighten.

The final item to check weekly (or daily, depending on engine time) is the alternator or generator belt. Actually, it should be checked every time you check the engine oil; and that doesn't mean once a season. If you are lucky, the belt will be easily accessible, but don't count on that. Some boatbuilders put the engine in first and then build the boat around it, such things as checking oil level become a major project; but most people never look for things like that at a boat show or even in the dealer's showroom. Too many are more concerned with how many bunks it has and what color the drapes are. When you are checking the belt look for two things: tightness and aging. When the alternator is doing heavy charging a tremendous strain is put on the belt. If it is too loose it will slip, which leads not only to low output, but excessive belt wear and early failure. If you adjust it too tight, you'll get excessive wear on the rotor end bearings. Just right is just tight enough not to slip. The minimum tension or pull on the belt should be 50 pounds, but that is impossible to measure without a special tool. Check by pushing on the belt with your thumb between the pulleys. If the belt deflects much more than one-half inch it is too loose, and should be tightened. While you are checking the belt, look on its inside, the bottom of the V. Check for cracking, glazing, peeling and separation of the belt from the reinforcing cords; all are signs of aging. If any of these things are happening, you need a new belt.

That's about all there is to do on a regular basis. Once a season I'd pull each of the fuses to check the end caps for corrosion and separation—caps occasionally come loose from the glass bodies. Then wipe them off with a rag or paper towel dampened with a shot of WD-40. Put the master battery switch to off and open up the control panel and carefully inspect the insides. Look for signs of corrosion (white powder) on the switches and terminals. Check for any loose connectors by wiggling the wires. While you have it apart, mentally trace around each of the circuits so you can see what each item is doing and what function it plays in the whole circuit. This part of your education will be invaluable next time you have to troubleshoot something.

With your curiosity aroused, go through your boat and look at each electrical device carefully. Those that have replaceable parts, such as bulbs, should be looked at first. Does the bulb merely unscrew from an exposed socket, like at home? Unscrew the bulb, check for corrosion on the base and put a dab of light oil or grease on the threads before screwing back in. I have seen one of these bases so corroded that the bulb broke while the owner was trying to unscrew it from the socket. Write down the type and wattage of each bulb for your inventory list. Do you have to remove a cover or globe to get at the bulb? If so, practice doing it before you really have to some dark and stormy night. How do you change the bulbs in your navigation lights? Can you do it from inside the cabin, or do you have to remove the whole light assembly from outside the cabin to get at the bulb? If so, that means rebedding it after changing the bulb. You never know for sure until you look. That's why you should do it now. Repeat the procedure for all the vessel's lights, even the ones up a mast. Someday you'll be glad you did.

Don't even think about taking electronics gear apart. There is nothing you are allowed to do to your radio, nothing you can do inside your loran or your depth sounder (except change an internal battery if you have one)—so stay out. But DO look for all the external fuses you can find, usually on the back of the case, check them and note the size and type of each. Also check the connectors for tightness and corrosion, and the wires for signs of chafing.

All this experience is completing or adding to your electrical education. Troubleshooting will be so much easier next time something doesn't work if you know where it is, how it works, and what it takes to fix it. Crawl into any unfamiliar places. Stick your head behind and under the bunks, poke your way behind the galley, feel down in the bilge, reach around and behind the engine. Trace a circuit by visually following the wires and touching them; if one seems to disappear some- where, where does it reappear? Are you sure it is the same wire? Don't be afraid to get your hands dirty or your knuckles skinned up, that's all part of the game.

So now, fellow skipper, you are on your own. You are ready to take on more responsibility for the upkeep and repair of your boat. My departing wish for you is smooth sailing, the strength to overcome adversity, the courage to face the unknown—and the challenge of a few interesting problems along the way.

## YOUR BOAT'S ELECTRICAL TOOL BOX

Your boat's tool box for electrical work should, or could in- clude some or all of the following items. These are ones I find handy to have aboard.

> Crimper tool—cuts wire, skins insulation, crimps terminals
> Diagonal cutting pliers—to cut wire, small size is OK
> Needle nose pliers—for holding parts and reaching into tight
>   places
> Small screwdriver—pocket size
> Continuity tester—purchased or homemade
> 12-volt test lamp—purchased or homemade
> Electric soldering iron or gun—rechargable model is handy;
>   so is 12-volt type
> Solder—rosin core only, thin wire melts easier
> Solder paste—no acid flux, CHECK!
> Multimeter—doesn't have to be too fancy
> Battery hydrometer and something to hold it
> Battery terminal puller

Battery carry strap
Flashlight
Some extra test leads with alligator clips
Pocket knife—Swiss Army, Boy Scout, etc.
Good set of the longest auto jumper cables you can find—just
    in case


## SPARE PARTS AND JUNK

In some convenient place on your boat find room for an electrical "junk box." Cardboard doesn't hold up very well on board because it gets soggy in time. This box will get heavier year by year, so get a substantial one of plastic or wood. Junk, as mechanics refer to it, is treasure—not trash. Many things will end up here, but you probably will want to start with some of these.

Collection of terminals and butt connectors. Start with an
    assortment kit, or a few blister packs of common sizes
Roll of plastic electrical tape
Roll of friction tape—for anti-chafe wrap
Light bulbs—a spare for each different type and size on
    board. Keep inventory up to date. Replace as used
Fuses—several spares for each size and type on board
A set of spare wire plug connectors—polarized are better,
    they plug together only one way
Plastic wire hangers or insulated clamps
Assorted lengths of hook-up wire—No. 16 AWG and bigger,
    as collected from jobs on board
Spare belt for alternator—may not fit in box, put in note with
    its on-board location
Most anything else electrical that is too good to throw away
    but is not really worth keeping ends up here

# Index

# HANDY ADDRESSES OF
# SOME COMPANIES MENTIONED

**American Boat and Yacht Council, Inc. (ABYC)**
P.O. Box 806
Amityville, NY 11701

**Battery Council International**
111 East Wacker Drive
Chicago, IL 60601

**Cole Hersee Co.**
20 Old Colony Avenue
South Boston, MA 02127

**The Guest Corp.**
17 Culbro Drive
West Hartford, CT 06110

**Wiring Device Division Harvey Hubbell, Inc.**
P.O. Box 3009
Bridgeport, CT 06605

**Marinetics Corp.**
P.O. Box 2676
Newport Beach, CA 92663

**Perko, Inc.**
16490 N.W. 13th Avenue
P.O. Box 64000-D
Miami, FL 33164

**Raritan Engineering Co., Inc.**
1025 N. High Street
Millville, NJ 08332

**Ray Jefferson, Division of Jetronic Industries, Inc.**
Main & Cotton Streets
Philadelphia, PA 19127

**Sailing Specialties, Inc.**
P.O. Box 527
Lexington Park, MD 20653

**Skipper Marine Electronics**
3170 Commercial Avenue
Northport, IL 60062
Call 1-800-621-1444

**Solar Power Corp.**
5 Executive Park Drive
Billerica, MA 01812

**Spa Creek Instrucment Co.**
616 Third Street
Annapolis, MD 21403

**Surrette Storage Battery Co.**
P.O. Box 3027
Salem, MA 01970

# INSTALLATION AND SERVICE RECORD

When you purchase and install any electrical items, record that information in this table. Keep all sales slips, warranty registration cards, owners manuals, wiring diagrams, and parts lists in a waterproof pouch stored on-board in a safe place. You may need them someday when you are off cruising far from home.

| Item | Serial Number | Date Purchased | Purchased From | Date Installed | Warranty Period |
|------|--------------|----------------|----------------|----------------|-----------------|
|      |              |                |                |                |                 |
|      |              |                |                |                |                 |
|      |              |                |                |                |                 |
|      |              |                |                |                |                 |
|      |              |                |                |                |                 |

# Service Record

Here is a handy place to keep a record of all maintenance and repair work done on your electrical and electronic equipment—by yourself as well as authorized technicians.

| Date | Service Performed | Comments |
|------|-------------------|----------|
|      |                   |          |

| Date | Service Performed | Comments |
| --- | --- | --- |
|  |  |  |

# NOTES

# NOTES

# NOTES

# NOTES

# NOTES

# NOTES

# NOTES